GO AND MAKE APPRENTICES

Go and Make Apprentices

PHILIP VOGEL

KINGSWAY PUBLICATIONS
EASTBOURNE

ISBN 0 86065 445 1

Biblical quotations are from the
New International Version, © New York International
Bible Society 1978.

Front cover design by Drummond Chapman

Printed in Great Britain for
KINGSWAY PUBLICATIONS LTD
Lottbridge Drove, Eastbourne, E. Sussex BN23 6NT by
Cox & Wyman Ltd, Reading.
Typeset by CST, Eastbourne, E. Sussex.

Contents

Acknowledgements

My thanks are due to my wife Hilary, who has been part of this book and has helped me to write it. To Anne who came to live with us and ended up typing the manuscript. My thanks also to Jim Holl, a friend and colleague, whose experience as a proofreader was a great help. Finally, I am grateful for Terry Brewer's contribution as an ex-apprentice (see the Appendix), and for all the other apprentices with whom I have been associated over the years, who have meant so much to me.

Foreword

Leadership must be one of the key words within the church today. Although there are undoubtedly several models which may be followed, and therefore an increasing number of books highlighting different stances in relation to leadership, I believe that this contribution from Philip Vogel is going to be of particular significance.

Not only has Phil touched on a subject that is close to the heart of many of us within the body of Christ, but he approaches the issues with a sensitivity and commitment borne out of many years of Christian service.

A background of diverse experiences is a necessary pre-requisite to facing such a large and important task. Phil's years at Millmead Baptist Church and then in Guildford Community Church have equipped him with an understanding of the nature of leadership in free churches of both an emergent, new type and from a more traditional perspective. His years as an evangelist have enabled him to see a variety of situations within this country which would be paralleled by few people within the church. His time within a community lifestyle has given him another unique perspective, while his years as Director of British Youth for Christ were a time of training and equipping younger leaders for ministry within both a national and local framework.

When you add to this more recent experience in guiding and directing leadership among emerging new churches, along with a church planting perspective, you really do have some semblance of 'all round ministry'.

Having known Phil for many years, I owe him a debt of gratitude, and it is therefore a great privilege to contribute a foreword to his book. When I graduated from London Bible College there were few who would have been prepared to take on a fairly angry, rebellious young man. Philip rarely feels threatened by that kind of challenge. In my own case, and in that of many others, he determined to build in foundations which would place us all in good stead for the years ahead. His sensitive perception of need and desire to recognize potential have meant that many are now serving God who, at least in human terms, would not otherwise have been doing so.

Within the pages of this book Philip looks at the kind of leader we need within our churches, at the ground for training, and the need to equip and support such leadership. He carefully examines some of the problems leaders face and gives to his subject a freshness of approach which make the book both readable and intelligent in its varied suggestions and ideas.

No one will agree with every page. No one who knows Philip would expect to do so! He will always present a radical set of alternatives. Yet few will be able to study these pages without sensing the determination of a man to walk with God and uncover those gifts of leadership which so often lay dormant within our churches.

I think you will be stimulated, challenged and encouraged, and I sense that to be Philip's concern in writing this book. May God give to each one of us the openness to change, a readiness to be confirmed in some of our existing viewpoints, and the potential to go forward in new directions as he leads us. Truly we live in a day when leadership has too often consisted of following a secular pattern. Alternatives are needed within the church. We need to learn from this book and others like it that have been borne out of experience from those who have been used by God to encourage and raise up leaders within this country.

Go and make apprentices is a theme that Philip has lived. It points in a direction which we need to recognize as strategic for the growth of the church in Britain today.

CLIVE CALVER
April 1986

Foreword

Can you teach an old dog new tricks? How does a doctor respond to taking a dose of his own medicine? Had I read this book without knowing Phil Vogel today, my enquiring, if not cynical mind would have certainly raised these questions and maybe others.

Over two years ago Phil, now turned fifty, joined Team Spirit, a ministry team which I lead. In many ways he is streets ahead of me in ability and experience, but God happened to anoint me for the leadership role. How would my old friend respond and cope with this situation?

I first met Phil in the early 60s. He was a great encouragement to me in ministry and in practical help. When he heard of my intention to 'go full time' he didn't pour cold water on my enthusiasm, warning me of all the pitfalls I would face, but built up my faith and trust in God. That was in 1967. Since then I've learned that Phil is not a sentimentalist—he's got strong opinions and feelings, and is not easily beaten in sport or in intellectual debate. So, in spite of my apprehension, I was uncertain as to whether I could handle him in the team and whether he would respond to my leadership.

My fears were totally unfounded. For while there have been occasions when it has been necessary for confrontation in our relationship, Phil has always yielded when the time for a decision came. He has been tremendously supportive and submissive without being a 'yes' man. I'm not quite sure how we got along without him. Phil Vogel is still at heart an apprentice, a true disciple of Jesus Christ. So read on with confidence.

JOHN NOBLE

I

Genesis

In the beginning—well, almost the beginning—my wife Hilary and I, complete with baby daughter, left our friends at a Christian community to live and work in Brighton and Hove.

That was 1961. We had married in 1958 and joined Christian Publicity Organisation, which was then a community where everyone put their possessions and money into a common purse from which all lived.

I had felt the call of God upon my life, and had a burning desire to preach the gospel and evangelize the world. All this seemed very distant as I struggled with relationships, wrapped bundles of *Challenge* newspapers, or dug gardens and ditches. I did not realize at the time that through these struggles I would learn much that would lay the foundation of my future understanding of the church and Christian living.

Relationships had to be worked through; it was unavoidable when we lived in such close proximity.

Attitudes towards possessions were quickly made apparent, especially when people were seen to be using or abusing what I considered to be mine. Faith was stretched as we learnt to trust God together for our needs, and attitudes towards authority were tested. It was one of those periods which, when I look back, I thank God for.

After three years at CPO, a new chapter in our lives began. We moved to Hove, where I had been seconded to work with a church whose pastor had asked for help.

The church was housed in a very large mission hall. The pastor had sought to make structural alterations so that the small congregation did not rattle in it like a handful of dried peas in a huge can, but it still seemed more empty than full. I remember walking into every room, some of which were damp, dirty and unused. I prayed to God, pleading that he would move by his Spirit and once again fill the place with his life and vibrancy.

(Some years later, in 1984, I was to experience the thrill of that prayer being answered. My good friend from those early days, Terry Virgo, invited me to stay overnight. On the Sunday morning I went with the family to Clarendon Church, which Terry was now leading, and saw the old place restored and filled to overflowing with people who were infused and enthused with the Spirit of God. I thanked God for the answer to my prayer. It had been a long time coming, but now I could see it was a reality.)

As I walked through the streets of Brighton and Hove in those early days, there seemed to be little to encourage me. I was reminded of Ezekiel's vision of the valley of dry bones. Spiritually the area seemed to be full of death and dryness, and I could imagine how Ezekiel must have felt when God asked him, 'Can these bones live?' (Ezek 37:3). Humanly speaking it seemed impossible and like Ezekiel I could only reply, 'O Sovereign Lord, you alone know' (Ezek 37:3).

Where was I to start? I had to begin somewhere. Slowly, so slowly that I hardly noticed, something began to happen which was to shape my whole future ministry. It began in this way.

I met a few young Christians who showed a keen desire to grow. I could see they needed to be drawn out and given an opportunity to develop, so we began to meet once a week in my home.

As I prayed about how to help this small group, I sensed the Lord leading me to Matthew 28:20, '. . . teaching them to obey everything I have commanded you.' So that was where I started. Everything I had begun to experience and obey from God I would pass on to these young Christians. In the meantime I would seek to experience more for myself.

This proved to be an exciting period of discovery and growth for us all. During the next three years we learned to praise God and pray together. We evangelized on a housing estate and on Brighton sea-front. One by one these young Christians were filled with the Spirit, and we began to experience his gifts to us.

Later, two of these young people gave up their careers and joined Hilary and me in serving God and 'living by faith'. One of them was Terry Virgo, who has since gone on to exercise an apostolic ministry which takes him all over the world. Keith Frampton was the other; for a number of years now he has had a leadership ministry as a missionary in Bolivia. In fact nearly all of that 'Monday night fellowship' went on to serve the Lord in some capacity.

It was not until some time later that I realized how closely I had followed a pattern. There had been about twelve of us who had formed the nucleus of our fellowship. I had taught and we had learned together for about three years, before moving on into different ministries. We had, in fact, followed the pattern that Jesus himself had set and then commanded his apostles to follow. It was then that I became aware that there was something very significant in discipling people as Jesus had done, and I have sought to work according to those same principles ever since.

Over the years I have learned a lot, mainly through mistakes, but as I have often said to my apprentices, 'Why not learn from my mistakes so you can learn in six months what it has taken me six years to learn?' I am now working with my own team and am also part of a larger group led by John Noble called 'Team Spirit'. I am helping church leaders (while at the same time learning myself), and I am still working along the same principles, many of which I am outlining in this book.

Primarily I am concerned to help develop leaders and ministries, but the principles can be applied at any stage of a Christian's life, whether it is training for leadership, or practical, everyday Christian living.

It has taken me twenty-seven years to learn these principles. I hope that by reading this book it will take you a considerably shorter time, and I hope that you will learn from my mistakes and improve upon my guidelines.

2

Go and Make Apprentices

'But where do we find the leaders?' the question
came not from the minister of a struggling church
with limited resources, but from one who led a
thriving church of several hundred members.
Many people in the church were businessmen and
women from teaching, medicine and other profes-
sions. In their daily lives they were in positions of
authority and responsibility, yet still the cry was:
'We don't have enough leaders for our church.'

This plea for leaders has been echoed again and
again on my visits to churches, both by those
wealthy middle-class areas and those on housing
estates and inner-city areas. Often that plea has
been a cry for help from those who are already in
leadership. A pastor of a church in eastern Europe,
harassed by the communist authorities and struggling with few resources, expressed to me his despair at not having others to share the burden of
leadership and ministry. Overloaded with responsibilities and pressurized by unreasonable demands

upon their time, such leaders and their families live under constant stress.

Does it really have to be like this? Do the responsibilities of leadership have to fall upon a select few overstretched men and women? Does the church not have many more potential leaders within its own ranks? Or is it that we are failing to recognize and develop such leaders?

My answer to the question: 'Where do we find the leaders?' is this: 'Leaders are not found—they are formed.' I am convinced that God has provided the potential for leadership and other ministries within his church. But in many cases this potential is simply not being realized. The crucial question is this: how do we recognize and develop that potential in order to meet the desperately growing need for leaders?

The future of the church will be determined by the quality of its leadership. A work is as good or as bad as its leadership. It will gain no grasp of God greater than that of its leaders. It will show no greater commitment or sacrifice than that demonstrated by its leaders. It will have no clearer vision of the purposes of God than those seen by its leaders.

A brief glance at the history of Israel will show how quickly the people of God could change, depending on the quality of the leadership. Gideon could change a backslidden, demoralized and defeated people into a victorious nation living under the rule of God. Yet they reverted just as quickly, prostituting themselves in idolatry, when Gideon died (Judg 8:33). This same pattern is reported time and time again in Israel's history. The spiri-

tual life of Israel could be measured by the spiritual
life of its leaders, and what has been true in the
history of Israel is equally true in the history of the
church. (As we shall see later, the test of an excellent leader lies as much in what happens after he
has gone as in the effects of his ministry at the time
of his leadership.)

My concern to nurture leaders has not sprung
just from my consideration of the history of Israel,
but also from the way that the Holy Spirit has been
moving in the church in recent years. The trend is
now a movement away from a 'one-man ministry'
where a man, usually a professional who is formally
trained and financially supported, is invested with
the responsibility of leadership, and considered to
be the only one able and gifted enough to minister
to the church. Instead the Spirit has revealed the
truth of the plurality of leadership, and many
churches are now being led by elders or their
equivalent.

The Spirit has also been leading us to appreciate
the diversity and distribution of gifts within the
church and the necessity of those gifts being in
operation if we are to see the body of Christ mature
(Eph 4:11-16). As a result there is a growing recognition of the ministry of apostles, prophets and
evangelists, not just pastors and teachers.

Another recent trend has been a mushrooming
of congregations. Hundreds of new churches have
sprung up in our land. Some of the larger churches
are breaking down into several congregations, and
home groups have become an established feature
in both the traditional churches and the so-called
house-church movement.

All these factors have promoted the increasing need for leaders. How to meet this need and how to develop leaders and ministries is therefore a vital question, and one which has occupied my thinking and ministry for many years.

It has been a great source of personal satisfaction to me that over the years I have been involved with a number of young men and women right at the beginning of their call and ministry in the kingdom of God. Starting in the early 60s in Brighton, through the period of time as Director of Youth for Christ, until more recently during my involvement at Guildford, God has brought me into the orbit of men and women (usually young but not exclusively so), whom I recognized had potential and gifts waiting to be developed and released in service for the kingdom. I have watched them grow in maturity and been challenged by their love and zeal for God. I have been alongside them and watched the tentative emerging of their ministries, witnessed their doubts and frustrations, and wept with them and for them in their times of despair.

For some I have grieved, because they never made it. For others I have been proud as I have watched them mature as men and women in Christ —strong and doing exploits, winning victories for the King and his kingdom.

A number of these men and women have encouraged me by speaking of the influence I had in those early formative days. Some have said this influence was fundamental in shaping their lives and ministries; others have said it was minimal, but it did strengthen them at that point in time. My work with these young people has been very rewarding and certainly the most satisfying aspect of my ministry. But it has not been simply a matter of personal satisfaction. The greatest thing has been to see how the kingdom of God has been enriched because the gifts of these men and women have been released into ministry.

It was Moody who said, 'I would rather put ten men to work than do the work of ten men,' an opinion to which every Christian leader would probably give a hearty 'amen'. However, the 'amen' could be followed just as quickly with the question, 'But how?' How do we put ten people to work? Whom do we choose, and how do we know that *God* has chosen them? How do we instil in them the desire to work? How do we train them? What attitudes should we adopt?

In the past I have been asked how all this can be achieved. I would pass off the question because I didn't really believe that anyone would be interested in what I had to offer, and I would flippantly reply, 'If I knew how it was done I would write a book about it.'

Yet when I thought more about it, I realized that there was nothing secretive or strange about how God had taught me and led me in these things. It had not been a mere coincidence that I had met a number of people who later developed into Christian leaders. Neither had it been solely due to some aspect of my personality. Rather, it was because somewhere in the early 60s in Brighton, more as a result of God's providence than diligent study, I stumbled across a biblical pattern which, when followed, would inevitably mean that men and women would be released into ministry. During the years this pattern has become clearer, and through trial and error my practice of it has developed, even though the basic principles remain the same.

The pattern is best expressed in the words of Jesus:

> Go and make disciples of all nations, baptizing them in the name of the Father and of the Son and of the Holy Spirit, and teaching them to obey everything I have commanded you. And surely I will be with you always, to the very end of the age (Mt 28:19-20).

The conclusion I have come to is that leaders and ministries are best developed by the process of discipling. Not all disciples of course will become leaders, but many more could—something I was soon to discover as I began to teach others what the Lord had taught me.

3

Go and Make What?

'Disciple' is one of those strange words which for most of us is only used in a Christian context. Occasionally we may hear of someone described as a disciple of Karl Marx or of some other philosopher, but generally the word has become the property of the church. Other words we use such as pastor, elder or deacon, are similarly strange to people's minds today. We do not use them in the business world or on the shop-floor. They are words that are rooted in the cultural life of biblical times, were freely used in the general course of life, and then adopted by the church to describe a function of its ministry.

It would be interesting to know what words would be used if the church began in our day and age, within our own culture. Would we talk about the 'board of directors' or 'councillors' to describe the function of elders? What word would we use to describe a pastor? I doubt if it would be shepherd, a word almost meaningless to the average town-dweller. It has been suggested that the word 'coach' would be more appropriate and understandable to describe the function of a pastor.

What term would we use for disciple? A student? But does that adequately describe the essential nature and function of a disciple? Today the word 'student' tends to be applied to someone undergoing formal education, learning by hearing lectures and studying books until he becomes qualified. This does not adequately describe what a disciple is or the way he is taught. The word 'learner' is more accurate. Most of us have had the experience of being a learner driver, and the way we have been instructed more closely resembles the way a disciple is taught.

How important is it that we use the word 'disciple'? If we know what a disciple really is, then it doesn't really matter if we don't use that exact term. The problem is that because the word is not in common use, we can either assume its meaning or make it mean what we want it to mean.

Some people have assumed that the word 'disciple' means 'super-Christian'. We have the twelve disciples who were apostles with a special calling and a particular ministry, therefore we have some Christians who are on a higher plane of commitment and ministry to whom those demanding conditions of discipleship apply (Lk 14:26-33). Meanwhile the rest of us ordinary, run-of-the-mill Christians can conveniently forget that all the followers of Jesus were called 'disciples' long before they were called 'Christians', and that those demanding conditions of discipleship apply to anyone who calls himself a Christian.

Just as dangerous as assuming a meaning is to make a word mean what we want it to mean. In that case the word 'disciple' is associated with a particular group or emphasis of teaching. Ever since Juan Carlos Ortiz wrote his book *Disciple* in 1975 the word has been thrust into increasing prominence. It has spawned books which have given rise to emphatic teaching and then teaching which would oppose such views. It has been so much used and abused, that rather like the word 'gay' it has largely lost its original meaning. In some circles it cannot be used at all because of the reactions it produces: 'Beware of the discipling movement,' some would warn. 'Be careful of heavy shepherding.'

This, I hasten to add, is hardly the fault of Juan Carlos Ortiz. He set the clock ticking by giving a necessary push to the pendulum; but as with any swinging pendulum there are those who want to give it an extra shove, and those who, threatened by the motion and afraid of where it might lead, try to stop it moving. It is not my intention to add to the controversy by pushing or stopping the pendulum, but simply to bring additional understanding to the meaning of being a disciple of Jesus. In doing this I hope not only to recover some of the word's true meaning, but also to enable us to fulfil the commands of Jesus.

What then is the best word to use to describe a disciple? Most scholars that I have consulted agree that the word most familiar to us, and that most aptly captures the essence of what it means to be a disciple, is 'apprentice'.

An apprentice, according to *Chambers Twentieth Century Dictionary* (1972), is one who is 'bound to another to learn a craft'. How appropriate that definition is for those who are disciples of Christ. They are bound to the Master by 'cords of love', as the old hymn says, learning the craft of knowing God, living out his life in us in service to him. An apprentice is one who learns his skill not only from reading books in the isolation of his study, but as he himself experiments and seeks to follow his Master. His confidence and ability grow through experience, until he becomes a fully-fledged master craftsman in his own right.

I saw this principle clearly illustrated when I was walking with my dog by the river one day. I watched a man trying to teach his children to row. He was walking along the path yelling instructions to his children who were in the boat, struggling to row. Although their effort was enormous, their strokes were badly timed. Consequently the direction of the boat and its progress were somewhat erratic; in fact, it went more or less round in circles. The father, who was growing more and more frustrated, began to demonstrate with his arms in the manner of a skilled oarsman. He knew precisely how it should be done, but whether by theory or experience I was not sure, because he was not demonstrating it where it mattered—in the boat! Some of the children then began to stand up and change places and argue about who should row and how. Disaster loomed but fortunately did not occur. As I stood watching this man on the bank, six feet away from the action, I was reminded of the common description of preachers, six feet above contradiction.

How often we preachers lay down what ought to

be done without demonstrating it or saying how. I have frequently asked groups of Christians, 'How many of you have been told that you should be witnesses?' Always a forest of hands goes up. But when I ask, 'How many of you have been taken out and shown how?' only three or four hands are raised.

I have found the same to be true in other disciplines of the Christian life. Too often as preachers we exhort people in what they ought to be doing, while inside the hearers there is the question, 'Yes, but how? Please show me.' This is not apprenticing people. Jesus said, 'Go and make apprentices.'

Earlier on my walk by the river that day I had seen another father teaching his child to row. The child sat between his father's legs, they both had their hands on the oars, they pulled together, and I could sense the child catching the rhythm as the oars moved backwards and forwards. The pleasure on both their faces was obvious, and what was also noticeable was that the boat was making excellent progress. That was true apprenticing.

4

Apprenticing—the Jesus Way

Apprenticeship—a well-established pattern of training

By taking disciples, or apprentices as I prefer to call them, Jesus was following a well-established pattern of training. In Old Testament times leaders had their apprentices. Joshua was the servant of Moses, serving his apprenticeship until he was ready to take over and become the leader of the people of God. Prophets also had their apprentices, Elisha serving under Elijah, for example.

Elisha saw himself as the successor to Elijah. In asking for the double portion, the right accorded to every elder son or heir-apparent, he would literally succeed to the mantle of the leading prophet to the nation. You can almost hear him saying to Elijah, 'Let others have their due inheritance as prophets, but as one chosen to be your apprentice, and having learned my craft well, let me be your successor.'

In New Testament times too, discipling was an

established way of training. Many rabbis would
have their band of disciples. These apprentices
would learn their skills by being constantly with
their rabbi. They would listen, observe and seek to
emulate the teaching imparted to them. They
would also serve their rabbi in practical ways, doing
numerous menial tasks—carrying the baggage, seeing to finances, buying food, paying taxes, preparing rooms for meals, carrying out errands. All the
time they would be growing in character and
understanding.

John the Baptist also had his disciples, men and
women who absorbed his teaching, learned how to
pray, carried out his errands and finally served him
by taking his body and burying it (Mt 14:12).

Discipling was not confined to religious groups
or to Jewish tradition. In Hellenistic culture, discipling was considered by the great teachers to be the
only true way of teaching. Philosophers before the
birth of Christ—men like Socrates, Plato and
Aristotle—taught this way. Each had a small, select
group of disciples who learned by sitting at the feet
of their teacher or by listening to their lectures in
shaded corridors.

Jewish boys would learn their trade by apprenticeship. Jesus would have learned carpentry this
way from Joseph, first as a small boy watching his
father at work, choosing and shaping wood to
make some household or agricultural implement.
Later he would have experimented and developed
his skills under the watchful eye of his father. He
was speaking from his experience as a master
craftsman when he said, 'My yoke is easy'
(Mt 11:30), meaning that it fitted perfectly and did

not chafe.

Jesus was born into a world where apprenticing was a well-established and generally accepted way of teaching and training, whether for religion, philosophy or trade. So it's not surprising to find Jesus following this established practice. However, he broke from the pattern in one noticeable way— he chose his disciples, they did not choose him.

'You did not choose me, but I chose you,' Jesus said (Jn 15:16). It was not for them to have the privilege of choosing whom they would prefer to follow; maybe the rabbi whose teaching sounded particularly palatable or pleasing, or one whose oratory might thrill the hearer, or another whose demands of service were less severe. It was too important a choice to be the personal preference of the individual, or even the collective mind of a larger company of believers. These men were to carry the future responsibility of the church, and as such they had to be chosen by God, a decision which could only come through much prayer.

I believe that if we would only follow more closely the examples of Jesus today, both in prayer and training, we would make far fewer mistakes over who is given leadership responsibility in our churches.

Apprenticeship not the only way

Although training through apprenticeship was part of the social and religious structure in the time of Jesus, let us not make the mistake of thinking that it was the only means of teaching and training and thereby the only option available. As there had been schools of prophets in Old Testament times, so in the days of Jesus and before, there were rabbinical schools for formal theological teaching.

I find it both interesting and significant to see that Jesus did not teach his followers and future leaders of the church by sending them to an existing rabbinical school or by starting one of his own. He chose to completely ignore this more formal method of training for a less formal and apparently more effective way.

It comes as an even greater surprise to realize that in our churches today we have chosen, to a large extent, to ignore the method which Jesus used and to adopt instead the method which he chose to ignore. Perhaps we have come to think that his way is not effective or applicable in our society, or we have placed too much emphasis on formal rather than informal training. By saying this I am not wishing to dismiss all aspects of formal training, but I do believe that we need to place a greater emphasis on apprenticing than we have done in latter years.

So why did Jesus choose this way of developing his leaders? We don't really know the answer to that question, and we can at best only speculate. One thing we can be sure of, however, is that this was not a choice determined simply by convention, circumstances or convenience. True, he was working within the tradition and convention of his day, but equally he was quite prepared to dismiss or go beyond the bounds of convention in order to convey God's truth. (Healing on the sabbath day is one example of this.)

The Scriptures indicate that as the number of

Jesus' followers increased, so it became more necessary for him to delegate authority. But I believe there was more to this decision than mere circumstance or convenience. There was something of far greater significance.

What advantage, then, would apprenticing have over other methods of teaching?

The word becoming flesh

Apprenticing follows a divine principle—the principle of the incarnation. John writes in his gospel of Jesus being the light of men (Jn 1:1-4). Man's light comes through life. The Word needed to become flesh and live among us for a while, so that we could see his glory.

How grateful I am that God did not simply dish out tracts of theological information about himself, imparting truth, concepts, precepts and doctrinal statements, and leave it at that. No, the truth of God became embodied in a person. Jesus said, '*I* am the way, the truth and the life' (Jn 14:6) not, 'This is the way.' Jesus was the living demonstration of truth to be seen as well as heard. 'Are you the one who was to come, or should we expect someone else?' (Mt 11:3) Jesus was asked by the disciples of John. The answer came, 'Go back and report to John what you hear and see.'

By taking a group of disciples with him, Jesus was able to demonstrate the truth of God in real situations. The disciples were able to relate to the heart and mind of God, to see the power and authority of a living God as Jesus rebuked demons and silenced storms. These experiences were to be the basis of their message to others. 'That which was from the beginning, which we have heard, which we have seen with our eyes, which we have looked at and our hands have touched—this we proclaim concerning the Word of Life' (1 Jn 1:1). How often we, as Christians, have been guilty of separating the word from life, thinking that to impart words is sufficient to bring light.

Jesus said, 'On this rock I will build my church' (Mt 16:18) and down through the ages controversy has arisen over what exactly Jesus meant by 'this rock'. Does it mean Peter, as Roman Catholics believe? Or is it the confession made by Peter, 'You are the Christ, the Son of the living God,' as maintained by the Protestant church?

The truth, I believe, is both. How can the church of Jesus Christ be built on people who do not believe and confess the truth concerning Christ? Recent statements by leading churchmen, apparently questioning the virgin birth and resurrection of Christ from the dead, only highlight the utter folly of assuming that because someone may be given authority and responsibility in the institutionalized church, the church of Jesus Christ is therefore being built on such men.

Equally, we are mistaken if we believe that the church will be built upon a statement of faith that is not related to a person. The church is being built upon living stones not just words. If the words are not related to life, it makes little difference how correct they are. The principle of the incarnation meant that Jesus could not be confined to a lecture room or library, but would need to be seen and heard, living out the truth of God and thereby teaching his followers.

Paul reinforced this principle when writing to the Thessalonians:

> Our gospel came to you not simply with words, but also with power, with the Holy Spirit and with deep conviction. You know how we lived among you for your sake. You became imitators of us and of the Lord; in spite of severe suffering, you welcomed the message with joy given by the Holy Spirit. And so you became a model to all the believers in Macedonia and Achaia (1 Thess 1:5-7).

I have often asked church leaders whether they would like their members to know the peace of God. They all reply that of course they would. I then tell them that the way is quite simple. They should follow the advice of Paul, and say to their people, 'Whatever you have learned or received or heard from me, or seen in me—put into practice. And the God of peace will be with you' (Phil 4:9). Teaching and training by apprenticeship gives a unique opportunity of following the same principle that is fundamental to the wonder of the incarnation.

Developing character

Jesus was concerned to develop character and right attitudes in the lives of those who were his followers and the future leaders of the church.

Many of the teachings Jesus gave to his disciples were centred on the nature of God—his love, power and mercy. The disciples saw these characteristics in Jesus as they lived and worked alongside him. Wrong attitudes or angry reactions from them earned them a rebuke but also an understanding of God's mercy. They learned about attitudes towards family, homes, money, giving, and relationships between leaders and led. The list of lessons is enormous, and they were learned with someone close at hand who would direct, correct and support them. As someone has aptly said, 'We are taught more from formation than from information.'

Preparing for the future

The selection of the twelve apostles, from a much larger group of disciples, is an important landmark in the ministry of Jesus. Coming approximately midway in the three years of Jesus' ministry, it marks the beginning of his preparation for the future leadership of the church. Until now he had worked single-handed and within quite a small area. If the kingdom was to continue and grow, Jesus would need men who were ready to take the responsibility of leadership after he had left.

Jesus was well aware that the choice of second and third generation leadership is often more critical than first generation. How often it has been true that a work has blossomed and grown under a man called and envisioned by God, and yet has declined when that man has left and the next generation of leaders has taken over. The true test of leadership would come after Jesus had left. The future of the kingdom would depend upon those men who were now apprentices to Jesus, and on how well he trained them. How much of his vision, his heart and his Spirit had been imparted to them? The answer to this question would be seen in the future leadership of the church.

Moses was a man called and empowered by God to lead a people out of slavery and on to establish a kingdom. Moses was not a short-sighted leader. He carefully prepared for the day he would leave by taking Joshua as his apprentice, preparing him for leadership of the nation, and thereby ensuring a smooth transition of leadership. Others who were to follow Moses were less far-sighted, it would seem. Inadequate preparation for future leadership led to eventual anarchy with everyone doing what was right in his own eyes (Judg 21:25).

In these days of what has been referred to as the 'charismatic movement', those of us involved face searching questions as to its future. Since the late 50s and early 60s, when this new move of the Spirit began to make an impact on the church, God has been pouring out his glorious 'new wine'. For some within the church, the taste of that wine was not good; they preferred what they were used to and remained with it. Others tasted it, thought it good, but tried to contain it within old, inflexible wineskins—the traditional forms and constitutions of established churches.

In many instances there has been a bursting of wine-skins, while others, seeing what has been happening, have prepared new and flexible skins for the wine. These apostles of God have foreseen the need for and have sought to prepare such new and flexible structures. To my mind they are undoubtedly 'first-generation' leaders in this recent move of God's Spirit.

But what of the next generation of leaders? Where and how are they being trained and prepared? Many of the original leaders in the charismatic movement were trained in the traditional way and have come with that experience into the new churches and fellowships which have mushroomed throughout the country. The more traditional way of training is not now considered the best way, neither is it the most practical, as many who are now taking leadership responsibility are unable to go away for formal instruction.

What then does the future hold? A leadership vacuum? An inadequate or immature leadership and an inevitable decline in growth? Quite possibly. Unless, that is, we follow the example chosen by Jesus.

Apprenticeship is not only the way chosen by Jesus, but also the way commanded by him—'Go and apprentice.' It is an explicit command issued by Jesus to his apostles.

As in the days of Jesus, so now there may be various options open to us as to how we teach and train those who come to believe in Jesus, and those who are to carry responsibilities in the kingdom. These options may be determined by convention, circumstances or convenience, but any option we choose, if it does not fulfil the objective of apprenticing people, is pointless and misguided. At its best such a choice would be ignorance, and at its worst, disobedience.

5

Apprenticing—the Goal

There was an old woman who lived in a shoe;
She had so many children she didn't know what to do.

I can sympathize with the poor woman—who
wouldn't! A harassed and distraught mum, trying
to provide for the needs of the children, giving
guidance here, exercising discipline there, sorting
out differences and squabbles and tears; cooking,
feeding, washing and, to boot (forgive the pun), it
was all happening in the most unsuitable accommodation.

I think a number of pastors and leaders of churches could identify with the old woman's problem.
Let's take a closer look at her problem and see if
there's any solution.

Better resources

First, let's consider the accommodation situation.
Would the answer be to move to more suitable
accommodation, swap a size five for a nine-and-a-

half broad fitting, so to speak? Or how about a pair of shoes instead of just one? It certainly would help, but the fact is that we tend to put a higher premium on material resources than we do on people resources or God resources.

This tendency to look to material resources for an answer can be seen in the twelve disciples of Jesus. Confronted by an overwhelming need to feed five thousand people, they were faced with Jesus' challenge not to send them away but to take the responsibility of feeding them (Mk 6:34-44). The disciples immediately thought in terms of material resources. 'That would take eight months of a man's wages! Are we to go and spend that much on bread and give it to them to eat?'

I doubt that they even had that much money. They were probably suffering from the 'if only' mentality that we so often adopt: 'If only we had more money, or better accommodation, or more resources, then we might be able to meet the need.' Jesus did not concern himself with what they did not have, but with what they did have, and they found that when they entrusted what little they did have into the hands of Jesus, it was more than sufficient to meet the need. I consider it an important and foundational principle that there are sufficient resources already present within the church to meet the demands that God wants us to meet at this moment in time.

Two lessons, one on feeding five thousand men, the other on feeding four thousand men, plus women and children (Mt 15:32-38), were enough to teach these apprentices where their resources lay. These lessons ensured that later, on the day of

Pentecost, when faced with an influx of thi
sand new believers, the disciples did not p.
send them away, but were enabled to 'fee
sheep'.

We may conclude, then, that the answer to the
old woman's problem is not to be found in a new
shoe, desirable though that may seem.

Birth control

Could the answer to a harassed mum's overcrowd-
ing problem be birth control? Would it not be more
sensible to limit the size of the family to that which
could be handled by the poor mother and her
resources?

I expect most of us would raise our hands in holy
horror at the mere suggestion that churches should
consciously limit their growth in any way. Yet that
is what, in practice, we do.

Churches tend to reach a plateau in their
growth, depending on accommodation, or on what
the leadership is able to cope with. When a new
church building is opened, numbers will often rise
quite rapidly, and then remain static when the
building is full. Subconsciously, we reach a similar
plateau in our faith and expectation for church
growth. At other times numbers will rise to what
the leadership can accommodate without too much
strain. Nothing is consciously said or determined,
but subconsciously the level is reached and the
work again remains on a plateau.

Campbell McAlpine recalls God speaking to a
church: 'I will give you as many sheep as you can
care for.' God is not frightened by large numbers.

In fact, he wants a very large family—people from every tribe and nation and language. Any mentality, subconscious or otherwise, which would limit the size and extent of his family must grieve God's heart.

It's a bit late in the day to talk to the old woman about what she should have done; she's already faced with the problem. I remember having to face this particular difficulty in one church where I was working. I listened to my friends, fellow leaders, telling me how they would not form a house group until they had a leader. Our problem was that we already had several hundred people and we could not tell them to go away for three years while we trained leaders. Somehow, like Jesus, we had to train and develop leadership while at the same time caring for the needs of all.

A father needed

Perhaps the woman's problem is the absence of a husband, a father-figure, a strong and mature person who could be respected and trusted, and had the experience and wisdom for running the shoe and everybody in it.

Since there is no one in the shoe at present with that ability, let's look around, invite one or two possibilities to speak to the family, and if we think one is suitable we'll import him to do the job. Maybe we'll even import a few more to help him.

This is the pattern that churches have adopted over the years, and I cannot deny that it has provided an answer to the problem. But the biggest drawback, in my opinion, is that it does not do a great deal in developing the maturity of the children. Surely we need to be thinking and working towards developing mature leaders from within, rather than continually relying on imported leaders. Imports should, I believe, be seen as a temporary necessity, until mature leadership is able to be developed from within, and responsibility under God is assumed.

This certainly seems to be the principle which the Apostle Paul followed. It is clearly illustrated by Titus' work in Crete. Titus, one of Paul's apostolic team, was left behind in Crete to consolidate the work and appoint elders, and then to join Paul once more (Tit 1:5). The appointing of elders seemed to be a significant stage in the new church's development. It was the point at which government of the local church became the responsibility of the local leaders, who were accountable first and foremost to God (Acts 20:28-36).

It is surprising to find how the relatively young in faith were given such responsibility. It would appear that elders were appointed in Lystra, Iconium, and Pisidian Antioch only a few months after they had become Christians. Although these elders would continue to need input, direction and teaching, nevertheless the responsibility for leading the church was now firmly with them.

All this seems to indicate to me that there is far more potential for leadership and ministry within our churches than most of us are prepared to recognize, and that the way to release this potential should greatly concern us.

Paul urges the Romans not to overestimate themselves, but to exercise sober judgement when evaluating gifts and ministries. The problem I share with so many Christians in Britain today is not that of overestimating but of underestimating and undervaluing our potential in God.

One day in January 1960 I came before God in tears. I was painfully conscious of my own inadequacies, and cried to God, 'Why me?' He spoke very clearly to me through Scripture in reply:

> For ye see your calling, brethren, how that not many wise men after the flesh, not many mighty, not many noble, are called: But God hath chosen the foolish things of the world to confound the wise; and God hath chosen the weak things of the world to confound the things which are mighty; And base things of the world and things which are despised, hath God chosen, yea, and things which are not, to bring to nought things that are: That no flesh should glory in his presence (1 Cor 1:26-29, AV).

I then challenged God to prove the truth of that scripture through someone like me, and since that day any success that I have enjoyed has come from God demonstrating that truth. Since that time I have been convinced that the key to the church's future is the realization of the potential in God that lies not so much in the few wise and mighty but in the majority who are considered to be weak and insignificant.

This leads me on to the other difficulty which I see in relying on 'imports'—it does seem to create an elite minority. There are few leaders who appear in the category called 'Super Star' by Howard Snyder in his book *The Problem of Wine-skins*. There are simply not enough of them to go round, and those who do go round (with a few exceptions) usually gravitate towards the more prestigious churches. Where does that leave the rest of us who by no stretch of the imagination could be called 'Super Stars'? And what does it mean for the future of the church if there are not enough of these people about?

Too many of us are left in the position of the man in Luke 19, whose master had given him a portion of money with which to trade. Unlike his colleagues he buried it, and when his master returned he was rebuked and punished (Lk 19:12-26). He buried the money because he had a completely wrong understanding of his master. But perhaps he also felt that he was not as gifted as his colleagues who had received much more, and therefore there was not much point in him trying to do anything.

God spoke to me one day concerning this parable, saying, 'The man could also have buried the money he was given because he was unaware of its value and didn't realize it could gain interest. He didn't really believe it would work out there in the market-place.' My response was, 'Yes, Lord, that sounds like me.' I felt the Lord reply, 'Don't you dare believe that what I have given you is not valuable. Don't bury it, put it to work.'

However, this problem is not just mine. We have a wealth of talent, experience and potential gifts buried in our churches, and because we do not believe that what we have is valuable enough to work, we are tempted to call in others to do it.

For those who, like myself, are keen football followers, a similar trend can be seen in the world of soccer. There the big names are enticed by the prestigious and wealthy clubs, with the result that these clubs then attract yet more talent, so the rich get richer and the poor get poorer. While the Hartlepools and Halifaxes of this world struggle on with limited resources, what talent they do have is likely to be creamed off by the Manchester Uniteds and the Liverpools. What are they to do? Casting envious eyes on the elite few will not ensure their survival any more than it will ensure the survival of struggling churches who cast envious eyes on the talents of their bigger brothers.

What are we to do in the similar situation in our churches? Jesus said, 'The people of this world are more shrewd in dealing with their own kind than are the people of the light' (Lk 16:8). This is certainly true of those who are successful in the less prestigious football clubs. They have succeeded by developing their own home-grown talent, and by persuading those with talent that there is a real future for them right there.

Too many children

Surely the real difficulty of this poor old mum is that all who are in the shoe, barring herself, are immature. Now, if a few—or even better—all of them were mature adults, able to take responsibility for their own lives, secure in their relationships, and able to contribute instead of constantly demanding attention, then the woman would be able to think about increasing the family.

The apostle Paul's goal for Christians is quite clear.

We proclaim him [Christ], admonishing and teaching

everyone with all wisdom, so that we may present everyone perfect in Christ. To this end I labour, struggling with all his energy, which so powerfully works in me (Col 1:28-29).

God's aim for the believer is maturity, and the provision he has made of gifts and ministries are for that end. They are given to prepare and repair (literally meaning to mend the nets) God's people for works of service so that the body may be built up and attain that goal of maturity (Eph 4:11-16). Just as it is the responsibility of every parent to prepare and guide their children towards maturity, so it is the responsibility of Christian leaders to disciple believers towards maturity.

The apprenticing that Jesus undertook produced mature people, apostles who were able to be the foundation of the church he was building. There is a lot taught today about discipling, much of which is good and beneficial. However, discipling that does not have maturity in Christ as its aim and accomplished result is a mere travesty of that demonstrated by Jesus and the apostle Paul.

How do we measure maturity?

Philo, the Greek philosopher, put his disciples into three categories: those just beginning; those making progress; and those beginning to reach maturity.

It is difficult to measure growth. Often it goes unnoticed because it is a slow process, or because we have no measure by which we can chart it.

A visitor might say, 'Hasn't your child grown

since I last saw him?' The parent may not have noticed particularly, unless there are some definite indications that growth has taken place. Perhaps bigger shoes have had to be bought, or trousers made longer. Maybe the parents have the heights of their children marked out on some wall with the appropriate date alongside. 'Isn't he big for his age?' Is he? How can we know unless we have some indication of an average-sized child?

It becomes even more difficult when we start talking not just of physical stature, but of maturity, and especially spiritual maturity. How do we measure maturity, and against what or whom? It is difficult. Even a puny, under-sized Englishman would look quite big in a tribe of pygmies, and I suspect that what often passes as maturity in our churches has been evaluated in this way.

The writer to the Hebrews speaks of leaving the elementary teachings about Christ and going on to maturity. He outlines what he considers to be the basic ABC of Christian understanding—repentance, faith in God, instructions about baptisms, laying on of hands, the resurrection of the dead, and eternal judgement (Heb 6:1-2). If people in our churches had a basic understanding of these things alone, we would consider them more likely to be in the sixth form rather than just emerging from the kindergarten.

What, then, is the measure of our spiritual maturity? It is the 'whole measure of the fulness of Christ' (Eph 4:13).

How do we measure this maturity? It is difficult to try and measure a person's growth from where they are to where they should be. The measure of

the fullness of Christ is one that we must all keep
before us, but at times it seems to stretch so far into
the distance as to make any growth that has taken
place imperceptible.

I find it a far more accurate indication of growth
to measure where a person has come from to
where they are now. Consider the Corinthian
church. If we look at where they were, compared to
where they had to get to, we would almost certainly
question whether any growth had taken place at all.
But if we look at the situation from which they had
come, then we see a more encouraging picture.
They still had a long way to go, but it was the position from which they had moved which showed
how much they had grown.

There are a lot of people in our society today
who are having to come from much further back
than people of my generation. Although I did not
believe in God before my conversion, at least it was
a Christian God I did not believe in, and my values
were basically Christian ones. This is not true of
most people today. Many who are becoming Christians are doing so from a position which has strik-
ing similarities to that of the early Christians in
Corinth.

How do we define maturity? For me, maturity
and responsibility are very much akin. To be
mature is to be responsible for my own life, for who
I am in God; for the decisions and choices of my
life; for my thoughts, actions, feelings and relationships. The extent to which a person can take such
responsibility shows the extent of that person's
maturity.

From this definition we can see that some forms

of discipling never bring maturity to believers, because they never encourage them to be truly and thoroughly responsible.

But when all is said, why is it that Christian leaders still find it difficult to produce maturity in others?

Maturity—a threat?

Do we really want to see people grow into maturity in Christ? Unfortunately, growth into maturity is not always welcomed by leaders. Sometimes it is perceived as a threat, especially if the leader is struggling with insecurities in his own life. Some churches are like some Christian homes I have visited. They are well ordered, with complacent but submissive children. Searching questions concerning dearly-held convictions, values and practices are not allowed. Such behaviour is seen as not being submissive to those in authority, or not honouring one's mother and father. Consequently, questions are suppressed under feelings of guilt for being 'rebellious', the status quo is maintained—but so is the immaturity of the believer. I am convinced that there is a direct relationship between a leader's constant appeal for submission to authority, his own insecurity and the immaturity of those he leads.

Overprotective leaders

The responsibility of leadership or parenthood is often difficult for Christians. We are genuinely concerned for the welfare of those we believe God has given us, but at the same time we are conscious of the dangers awaiting the unwary or the inno-cent. Christian leaders, on the whole, take seriously their responsibility to guard the flock of God (Acts 20:28). But all too easily leaders, like parents, can become overprotective and overrestrictive towards those for whom they care. Because we are anxious our children should make the right decisions and the right choices, we end up making the decisions for them—all of course for their best interest. Commendable though this desire may be, what can result is that when the children have grown up and have to make responsible decisions for themselves, they are unable to do so.

An elder once talked to me about the 'heavy responsibility' of having to make decisions for those in his care. I responded by questioning if that is really what an elder is supposed to do.

As a rule, I don't encourage people to come to me for decisions. It's not that I don't care about the choices people have to make, it's that I want to help them to learn how to make those choices in the right kind of way. I want to help people to hear God for themselves, and my part in this process is to help them to clarify issues and the right data so that they do not have to be constantly coming back to me for answers.

I remember one time when my son Stephen came to me for help with his homework. It was not very often I could supply the answer, but this piece of work was for Religious Education so I was at least supposed to know the answer. As it happened I did know, but I did not simply give the answer to Stephen. Instead I helped to show him the different views, showed him where he could get some more information and left him to come to his own conclusion. Interestingly enough, when his teacher commended him for his work and asked him who had helped him, he replied truthfully that no one had. He genuinely felt he was responsible for the conclusion he had reached, and of course to a large degree he was. I had simply played my part as a teacher/discipler, bringing him further along the road to complete maturity.

Anxiety and fear

A leader's own anxieties and fears often prevent others from maturing. How many of us parents have had to battle with our fears and and anxieties as we have watched our children enter adolescence? How they behaved, what they wore and which meetings or clubs they attended were areas which had once been under our control. The values they accepted were our responsibility to shape, albeit gently and persuasively. When they were told to sit, they sat—even if they did it like my dog who sits at my command though he's often still standing inside.

But as our children grow into adolescence they question and rebel; if they want to stand, then they stand—unless they can be shown it is in their interest to sit. Our control over their maturing life slowly but inevitably slips away. What had once been our responsibility gradually becomes theirs, even though at first they are not able to be fully responsible.

What do we do? If you're like me, you'll grit your

teeth, shut your eyes, trust God and let go. But if we allow fears, anxieties and insecurities to predominate, we become overprotective towards our children, holding them back in childhood in the 'safety' of our control. But by doing this we restrict their growth.

If we want people to mature in Christ, we must recognize adolescence as a very positive and necessary transition period in their development. As leaders, we must deal with our own insecurities, fears and anxieties so that we can release others to assume responsibility for their own lives, thus creating opportunities for them to mature. I have found in Christian leadership, as I have found with my own children, that most people are able to assume responsibility far sooner than I am prepared to give it.

Chinese footbinding

You are probably familiar with this old Chinese custom. The feet of little Chinese girls were tightly bound from birth because ladies with very small feet were considered to be attractive. Severely restricted growth, deformities, and inability to walk freely were the high cost of producing something that was culturally attractive. Unfortunately, we have done the same thing in our churches. We have often been guilty of sanctifying our culture, making theological issues out of what are basically cultural ones. We have done it in matters of dress, music, the way we behave in our services and the way in which we teach and train.

Attitudes towards dance in worship illustrate this point. Most objections to the use of dance in wor-

ship stem from our culture which has been greatly
influenced by Greek philosophy. This philosophy
considered things of the body to be bad and only
things of the spirit to be good. Things of the body
—food, sex, money, dance, etc.—were labelled 'secular', and considered to be beyond the reach of
sanctification. How different from Jewish philosophy that considers the whole of life as worthy of
sanctification by God. We can eat, dance, work,
give, spend, and make love as husband and wife—
all to the glory of God.

I would also say that I suspect that quite a lot of
what I have observed as dancing in our churches of
recent years, owes much to our culture as well as
the spirit. The disco dancing culture of our age has
found expression in our worship, and I have seen
how this can be done naturally, without offence.

For the most part, God is mindful of our culture
and works within it. The problem comes when a
church fails to distinguish between that which is
cultural and changing and that which is theological
and unchanging. The church then becomes 'cul-
ture-bound', and the result is just as restricting as
Chinese footbinding. The church may be culturally
acceptable, but in actual fact it is an ugly deformity
instead of God's original design. If we are to see
true growth in people's lives, then there must be a
loosening on earth as well as in heaven.

Maturity in Christ is high on God's programme.
He is not simply wanting to populate the kingdom
with babes in Christ, and certainly not with those
who are still babes long after they should have
grown up.

There is nothing wrong with being a baby—we

all start that way both physically and spiritually. What is tragic is when a baby does not mature. How sad it is to see a person with a grown-up body, but who still has the mind and emotions of a child. It must sadden God even more to see Christians of some years' standing who are still childish in their understanding and in their relationships, and very unsteady on their feet when they should be walking and running.

We have seen that growth is a natural process which must be fostered or can be hindered. Let's consider this in greater depth.

The right environment

No one is going to grow unless they are in an environment that will encourage growth.

Adam was placed in a garden. There he felt valued and significant, and he enjoyed God's approval. In addition to all this he was given a task in which he could find fulfilment, boundaries within which he could feel secure and relationships in which he could experience love and affection. All these things formed the perfect environment in which man could grow and find his true maturity. When Adam and Eve sinned, they opened the way for the ruination of that environment. All the signs of insecurity that man has come to know so well began to show—shame, the cover-up, hiding away because of fear and blaming everyone except yourself. It all went horribly wrong for Adam and Eve. Instead of reaching their full stature they shrivelled into a caricature of their true selves. Ever since that time men and women have lived in that caricature and have looked for a garden where they can grow.

We need a place where we can feel significant, where we are valued and, above all, where we can feel the sense of God's approval upon our lives. If we fail to find that place, then we try to find that value and approval in the tasks that we do, the boundaries that we impose (a form of legalism), or the relationships to which we cling like leeches.

Blessed are those who know God's value and approval on their lives, for they shall know no fear.

Blessed are those who are doing the task that God has given them, for they will find fulfilment.

Blessed are those who live contentedly within God's boundaries, for they will not experience frustration.

Blessed are those who are loved, accepted and forgiven by their brothers and sisters in Christ, even as they are by Christ himself, for they shall know security.

Blessed are these people, for they have found a garden where they can grow.

Do we want to grow?

Even though we may live in an environment where growth can take place, we still have to determine to grow. 'What do you want me to do for you?' This question was asked by Jesus to two blind men who cried out to him (Mt 20:29-34). Surely their need was obvious. Wasn't Jesus aware of their condition? Of course he was, but they still needed to take some responsibility for their healing by specifically voicing the desire of their heart.

'Why have you come to see me?' I asked a young man who had come to see me. 'Because my elder told me that I needed to receive your counsel,' he replied. I told him to come back when he could let me know what *he* felt he needed.

Do we really want to grow? We will know little progress until we make a clear decision to grow, and act with determination. This means we have to take responsibility for our growth.

A few months ago I was feeling distinctly unhappy about various issues in my church. I had handed over leadership to one of my apprentices. I had been released to do work outside the fellowship and was financially supported in my new venture. However, there were certain things in the church which I felt were being done that ought not to be done, and other things not being done that ought to be done. I became more and more unhappy. Perhaps it would be better if I left altogether?

I was aware, though, that issues are very rarely—if ever—the problem. They are pegs on which we hang our problems. So I was keen to find out from God what exactly my problem was. He showed me that I no longer felt wanted. Having identified my problem and taken responsibility for it, I was soon able to deal with it. The issues that had been bothering me were no longer a problem.

In our determination to grow we must understand that there is no real growth without pain: 'Suffering produces perseverance; perseverance, character; and character, hope' (Rom 5:3-4). We live in a society that is committed to taking the pain out of life, yet the truth is that to grow to maturity

in Christ is a painful experience. We seek to anaes-
thetize ourselves against all pain, from birth to
death. We have fashioned a God for ourselves who
exists to make life comfortable, easy and pain-free.
The result is immaturity and shallow relationships
between man and God, and between man and man.

If we are to see growth take place, then we must
instil a determination to grow and also ensure that
hindrances to growth are removed.

Hindrances to growth

In my experience of helping people in their growth
in God, I have come across the following areas of
hindrance.

Sin

I suppose that this is the most obvious hindrance to
growth. Unforgiven and unresolved sin acts like a
tourniquet on a life-giving artery, it stems the flow
of the Spirit and leads to a gradual stunting and
withering of growth. Just a cursory glance at the
cross will show that sin cannot be dismissed, ignored or excused—it has to be resolved.

Resolving sin involves repentance, which is a different matter from remorse. People are often confused between the two. Remorse is a matter of
conscience, involving feelings of sorrow sometimes
expressed with tears. King Saul was full of remorse
over his behaviour towards David (1 Sam: 24:16-
21; 26:21-25), but he was not repentant for he did
not change his mind.

2 Corinthians 7:8-12 shows the difference between worldly sorrow and godly repentance. The
repentant mind is reflected in the attitudes that the

Corinthians showed: an eagerness to put matters right, an indignation, alarm, and an earnest concern to see righteousness and justice done. People who learn to take sin seriously are people who will grow.

I remember a man sitting in a meeting at which I was speaking. He was shouting, 'Hallelujah,' and, 'Praise the Lord,' at various points during my message. Normally I find this helpful, but on this occasion there was something not quite right about it, so afterwards I sought him out. He told me that he had been doing it 'to get back into the Spirit'. When I asked him what had taken him out of the Spirit in the first place, he told me about his sin. I pointed out to him that no amount of 'hallelujahs' and 'praise the Lords' would deal with his unresolved sin and I showed him 1 John 1:9. Even then he did not seem to understand, for he started to appeal to God for forgiveness. As a rule I do not like to interrupt people when they are talking to Father, but in this instance I felt I had to do so. I told him that he did not have to beg God for his forgiveness, because he had promised it already if we confess our sin.

Forgiving others

I used to think God's forgiveness was like his love—unconditional, but I gradually changed my mind as I came across scriptures such as Matthew 6:14-15. Jesus told a powerful story to teach the necessity of forgiving others. Once there was a king who cancelled the debts of a servant who owed him a great deal of money. But when this servant refused to cancel the debts of a fellow worker who only owed

him a very little, the king had him thrown into jail.
A clear message is derived from this parable—our
heavenly Father will treat us as the king treated the
harsh servant, unless we forgive our brothers and
sisters from our hearts (Mt 23-35).

We who are freely forgiven are so quick to pass
judgement on others. Either we pass a suspended
sentence on them: 'I will turn the other cheek this
time, but watch out, I only have two cheeks!' or else
we lock them up in our prison of judgement,
usually throwing the key away. And there they stay,
without much hope of redemption. But in his parable Jesus shows that it is not just the offender who
gets imprisoned but also the offended. His experience of release and the joy of being forgiven are
lost when he fails to forgive others.

It's more than probable that a person is hindered
in their spiritual growth because they are withhold-
ing forgiveness for another. They will need to release the hidden resentment, thus releasing the
offender, so that both offender and offended can
walk free.

Restoring the years

Mark 3:1-5 recounts Jesus' healing of the man with
a shrivelled hand. I have often wondered what had
caused that man's hand to shrivel. Had he literally
played with fire? Had he touched things he should
have avoided? Or was his injury the premeditated
or thoughtless action of another? Perhaps he was
just born like it. We shall never know the cause, but
the result is in no doubt: his hand was shrivelled
instead of being whole and healthy.

No doubt over the years the man had learnt to

live with his injury, adjusting his way of doing things in order to cope with having only one strong hand. I have become only too aware in my own life and the lives of those I have sought to help over the years how we try to adjust to living with emotional wounds. Rejection by our parents, the loss of a loved one, a traumatic experience which has scarred us, the lies we have believed about our self-worth, lack of love. . . . The list seems to be endless. But the elements within it share a common characteristic—they inflict hurts in our lives which can affect our growth into wholeness and maturity.

We learn to live with these things. It's rather like when we get a stone in our shoe and we become adept at wriggling it around so that it doesn't hurt too much. We forget about it until it comes under extra pressure, then suddenly we feel a surge of pain.

The marvellous thing I have discovered over the past ten years is that God wants to take the stone out. That may seem obvious to you, but it wasn't to me. I had been trying to help people with their hurts by helping them to adjust to their injury. Although I realized that many of them had been hurt in the past, sometimes way back in childhood, we were in the present. It was as if we were locked in time. It was only when I gained a more vital understanding of the truth that God is not locked in time but is the 'I am' of yesterday and tomorrow, that I grasped that he can deal with the hurts of the past as if they had happened today.

The first man who came to see me after I had come to this understanding was distraught with remorse. He had been troubled for many years with a sexual problem that had brought him into the courts. He could see suicide as the only means of escape. As we prayed together, God revealed to me that he had been sexually abused as a child by his neighbour. I brought healing and release in Jesus' name to that child and he was set free. Several weeks later he told me that he hadn't known a day in seventeen years when he had not grappled with temptation, but now he was totally free from it. I have seen many other hurt people wonderfully healed, though not all have been as severely hurt as that man. Their lives have known the fulfilment of God's marvellous promise: 'I will repay you for the years the locusts have eaten' (Joel 2:25).

The enemy of growth

Satan is quick to gain a foothold on our lives, to limit and bind us, especially if we, or members of our family, have wandered into his territory and become involved in the occult. Ignorance is no safeguard and neutrality is not acknowledged by Satan. To wander foolishly into his domain is to run the risk of being attacked and ensnared. Too often I have come across a blockage in a person's life that does not shift through the normal means of counselling. I then begin to explore any possible involvement with the occult, either by the person concerned or in their family history.

Paul writes about demolishing strongholds by divine power (2 Cor 10:3-6). A stronghold is a well-established, strongly-defended fortress that guards the entrance to a territory or an important trade route. Jericho controlled the entrance to Canaan. Megiddo controlled the trade routes from Asia,

Africa and Europe. Whoever controlled the stronghold held the key to the land and the trade that could pass through it.

Strongholds cannot be bypassed or ignored. Gaza, Gath and Ashdod were strongholds ignored by Joshua (Josh 11:22). An examination of their history shows that this was a fatal mistake. Gaza was the city from which Delilah came (Judg 16:1); Gath was home to Goliath (1 Sam 17:4); and Ashdod was the site of the Temple of Dagon where the Philistines took the captured Ark of the Covenant.

No, we cannot afford to leave strongholds in the control of Satan. Jesus said, 'The prince of this world is coming. He has no hold on me' (Jn 14:30). If we are to see people grow, strongholds have to be demolished.

6

Apprenticing—the Call

As I have stated earlier, it was midway through the ministry of Jesus that he called twelve men from the large group that followed him (Lk 6:12-16). These men were called to be trained and equipped for a specific responsibility and ministry. I see from this that there is a specific call of God, as well as a general call of God.

The general call is the one God gives through the gospel. Peter preached at Pentecost:

> Repent and be baptised, every one of you, in the name of Jesus Christ so that your sins may be forgiven. And you will receive the gift of the Holy Spirit. The promise is for you and your children and for all who are far off—for all whom the Lord our God will call (Acts 2:38-39).

Paul also writes of the calling of God through the gospel, to share in our Lord Jesus Christ (2 Thess 2:14).

There are also more specific calls. God calls men and women to be married or single (1 Cor 7:17).

Then there is the call of God to a particular ministry and responsibility within the church, as in the case of the apostles. It is sad that we have made both too much and too little of this calling.

Making too much of the call

We have made too much of the calling of God to a particular ministry and responsibility by limiting it to a select few who have been 'called' by God to minister to him and one another. We have enshrined this misconception by establishing clericalism with its special dress and titles, and by the way we conduct our services and organize the structure of our churches.

This is what John Stott has referred to in his book *One People* (Falcon Books) as the 'scandal of clericalism'. He writes:

> What clericalism always does, by concentrating power and privilege in the hands of the clergy, is at least to obscure, and at worst annul, the essential oneness of the people of God. Extreme forms of clericalism dare to re-introduce the notion of privilege into the only human community in which it has been abolished. Where Christ has made one, the clerical mind makes two again, the one higher, the other lower, the one active, the other passive, the one really important, because vital to the life of the Church, the other not vital and therefore less important. I do not hesitate to say, that to interpret the Church in terms of privilege, clerical cast, or hierarchical structure, is to destroy the New Testament doctrine of the Church. [Page 21.]

These are strong words which, if heeded, would bring a revolution to church life, and a liberation of ministries. There may be some of us in apparently less clerical settings who feel that because we are not operating within the familiar forms of clericalism that we have avoided its pitfalls. We should take a closer look, for too often it is a case of 'same meat—different gravy'.

Another danger of making too much of the call is to equate it with being 'qualified'. Just a cursory glance at the call of the twelve reveals that this is not so. They were just at the beginning of their training. There was still much preparation to be done, lessons to be learned, character to be formed and attitudes to be changed. Later, eleven of the twelve would 'qualify' and be ready to assume responsibility in the church, but they were in no way ready when they were first called.

How I wish that this principle had been grasped in the early days of my ministry. I was certain of my call yet obviously nowhere near being qualified and able. It seemed at times that I was expected to be qualified and able because I was called, while at other times my call was in question because I was unqualified. Both situations created real heartache and heart-searching for me.

We must recognize the importance of a distinctive call of God in a person's life, but in so doing realize that we are dealing only with a potential leader. I have made the mistake, and I am sure others have also, of appointing potential leaders into actual leadership, with disappointing and frustrating results when the potential is not realized. I have also learned the lesson that it is much more difficult to 'unappoint' people than to appoint them.

'Do not be hasty in the laying on of hands,' is singularly good advice in this respect (1 Tim 5:22). I believe it is right to give full recognition to the call of God in a person's life, and at the same time bring them into apprenticeship in order to develop and realize that potential, and avoid the danger of equating being called with being qualified.

Finally, let us not separate the call from the one who is called. It is so easy to concentrate on the ministry and neglect the one who is ministering. Many people may recognize and applaud the gift and performance of an outstanding musician. He himself concentrates on developing his gift and practising to perfection, but his gift may well become more developed than his character. People respond to his gift and stand in awe of him, but they fail to recognize the needs of the person behind the gift. Eventually he only finds his value in his gift, and others value him for the same reason. Sadly for him, and for us, when his gift declines so does his value—in the eyes of other people, and his own.

Similarly in the church, we can come to relate to and value people primarily for their gift and ministry. I have often seen churches who relate to their minister only on a functional level, valuing him for what he provides. It's rather like the way we relate to our milkman—as long as he delivers the goods and doesn't wake us up too early we are satisfied, but if he fails to produce the cream that we are depending on then we will change him for another. The fact that he might be suffering in some way with personal needs doesn't really occur to us. No, we expect the goods to be delivered—after all, that's what we pay for.

I remember a pastor speaking to me once about his 'public face' and his 'private face'. His public face was one of ministering week by week to the needs of others. His private face was that of a grieving father in an anguish of guilt and concern over the mental health of his daughter. I do not know whether he was unable to let his private face be seen in public, or whether the church would not allow it. Either way, his predicament highlights the danger of separating the call from the one who is called.

How relieved I am to be among a people who see differently. Having been given a three months' break by the church, I came back somewhat nervously to my colleagues, who are also my friends, saying, 'I just don't feel ready to start again.' Their immediate response was, 'That's fine, take your time, we'll manage.' They have seen so often and so clearly that I am more important than my calling. We must never make so much of the call that we neglect the person.

Making too little of the call

However, we must be careful not to go to the other extreme, for failing to recognize a call of God to a specific ministry creates disorderliness and great frustration. People in the church do not know who is responsible for what, so nothing gets done. Alternatively, people become very overworked and pressurized, trying to complete tasks which God never intended them to undertake.

The other danger I see in making too little of

God's call to the ministry is being given responsibilities on the basis of qualifications.

If we ask ourselves what was the basis on which
Jesus called his twelve apostles, we're hard-pressed
to find a particular virtue common to them all. Certainly it was not education, character or previous
experience. True, they were devoted to Jesus and
enthusiastic for the kingdom of God, but no doubt
so too were countless others who were not called in
that way. No, the simple answer, as Mark records,
is that Jesus 'called to him those he wanted'. It was
purely his sovereign choice (Mk 3:13).

It is true that character is essential in the one who
is called. As Paul writes to Timothy concerning
elders and deacons, a man must be able to manage
his own life and that of his family before he is able
to take charge of the church (1 Tim 3:12-13). However, let us not ignore the fact that those qualities
of character are required of all Christian men, not
just elders and deacons. Character is given more
priority than ability in the list of some twenty qualities for elders which Paul outlined for Timothy
and Titus. In fact, the only ability mentioned is that
of teaching. All the other requirements concern
character.

Some may be in a similar situation to one church
whose leaders I was talking to. They had men who
were qualified in character and ability to be elders,
but their problem was how to recognize which ones
were called by God.

To me, recognizing the call of God is extremely
important. As Director of British Youth for Christ
I had to interview young men and women who
wished to join the work. I would say to them, 'I

want to establish one thing, and that is whether or
not you are called by God. I don't care if you can't
read or write, that is something I can teach you to
do, but I cannot teach you to be called by God.'
Why did I consider the call so important? I knew
that if these young people were called, God would
also equip them. I knew, too, that they were likely
to be committed to fulfilling the call of God on
their lives.

There have been times in my ministry when
there has seemed to be no way forward. Circumstances have risen up against me, and even Christians who I thought would understand have seem-
ingly discouraged me. At those times I have held
onto two certainties—belief in God, and his call on
my life.

How can we recognize when God is calling certain people to be apprenticed for leadership and
ministry? I wish I knew. I wish there was some
foolproof way or checklist that would guarantee
against mistakes. So much heartache and pain
could then be avoided. Paul and Barnabas could
not agree about Mark. Paul was right to choose
Timothy, but Demas was a big disappointment to
him. Let's face it, we are going to make mistakes.
Certainly I have. However, I believe I can learn
from my experience and make a checklist of my
own.

We should never lose sight of the fact that the
harvest field is the Lord's and it is his prerogative to
choose the workers for it. Jesus commands us: 'Ask
the Lord of the harvest, therefore, to send out
workers into his harvest field' (Mt 9:38), and he set
us an example by spending all night in prayer seek-

ing his Father's will before choosing the twelve apostles. I have tried to obey his command and follow his example throughout my ministry. When I have needed workers I have asked God for them, and he has supplied them. The Christian world has its own stock of advisers, consultants, managers and foremen but, alas, not that many labourers. I have noticed that when God sends someone into the harvest field they are really prepared to work.

Know your apprentice

One of the difficulties of importing a leader from outside the fellowship, especially where there is little or no established relationship, is that your understanding of that person will be limited. It is far easier to recognize the call of God on a person's life and have some awareness of their character when you have been in a fairly close relationship over a period of time. You are then able to see them in a much more realistic setting and are therefore able to assess whether there is a real basis for the call, rather than a passing fancy or a search for status and value.

Faithful and able

Paul commands Timothy to choose those who are both faithful and able (2 Tim 2:2). There are men in the church who are extremely faithful but not able, and others who are able but not faithful. Paul was on the look-out for men who were faithful in their walk with God, and reliable and loyal in their service for him. They would not serve him just because there are people watching who could give them admiration and applause, but simply because they are faithful.

I believe that Paul also included loyalty to others within the category of faithfulness. A man who is not loyal to others will not be loyal to God. Qualities of character do not include within themselves separate compartments, some of which apply to our own relationship with God and differ from those which apply to our brothers and sisters in Christ. In this day and age, loyalty is not a quality that is particularly admired or observed. Faithlessness in marriage has reached such epidemic proportions that those who do remain faithful to their partners seem to be a rarity.

In a world where loyalty seems to count for little, and at best is very fragile (whether in friendship, family or at work), perhaps it is not surprising that it seems to be a rather withered fruit in the church. But it is sad.

The kind of loyalty Paul had in mind is shown by Noah's sons, Shem and Japheth. Noah foolishly got drunk and then lay naked on his bed. Ham came out and talked about it, so Shem and Japheth went in with their eyes averted and covered Noah's nakedness (Gen 9:20-23). Their loyalty to their father would not allow them to make capital out of his weakness and foolishness.

True loyalty does not cover over unrighteousness for the sake of peace and quiet. To do that would be unfaithful to God and unhelpful to the person who was doing wrong. True loyalty was shown by David to King Saul.

While Saul was maliciously pursuing David, intending to kill him, he found himself in a situation where he was entirely at the mercy of David. Urged by his men to kill Saul, David crept up on him while he was asleep. No one would have blamed him had he plunged the dagger right into Saul's heart; he could well have justified his action. Instead, he cut off the corner of Saul's robe and slipped away unnoticed. Even though he had not harmed Saul, David was still conscience-stricken for having cut the robe of the King:

> The Lord forbid that I should do such a thing to my master, the Lord's anointed, or lift my hand against him; for he is the anointed of the Lord (1 Sam 24: 1-6).

I wonder how safe people are with us? We're highly unlikely to stab a person who's wronged us, but we often cut a little corner off their reputation. I cringe when people come to me saying, 'My pastor's a lovely man really and he means well, but . . .', and out comes the criticism. They are what my dear friend Denis Clark used to call nanny-goat Christians, always ready with a but. Unless he could stop the conversation before they got to the 'but' he knew that his view of the person under criticism would be affected because they had had a corner cut from their reputation.

I remember how a number of years ago, when I had an itinerant ministry, people would discuss the ministry and personality of others who also travelled round the country. There was one particular man, greatly used by God, to whom I found I had a growing dislike, yet I had never met him. When I

questioned myself as to why this should be, I realized that people had been cutting corners off the
robe of his reputation by their manner of talking
about him. By the time I met this man he was prac-
tically naked. I am delighted to say, however, that I
found him to be far different from the reputation
others had given me to believe.

Loyalty is not a natural fruit of the human heart,
but part of the fruit of the Spirit (Gal 5:22). It
needs to be nurtured and valued, for it is a very
rare and precious commodity.

Loyalty begets loyalty, and a leader cannot expect loyalty from those to whom he does not show
it. I have spoken to school-teachers who do not feel
that they have the loyalty and support of their
head-teacher. They do not know if they will receive
his backing in matters of discipline, or disputes
with parents. The teachers tell me of the insecurity
of their position and the near impossibility of their
task. This inevitably leads to a loss of morale and
commitment to the job in hand.

I have been amazed at the loyalty shown by a
number of apprentices that I have had with me
over the years. I remember speaking to one and
asking him why this was so. He replied that it was
because I was loyal to him. This surprised me at the
time, but I have come to realize the truth of it since.
I have tried to be loyal to and supportive of those I
am apprenticing, especially when they have made
mistakes. After all, I reasoned, if I benefit and receive credit when they do well, I should also be
prepared to shoulder some of the responsibility
when they do wrong. If we want to see loyalty—or
any other quality—in others, there is one simple

way to obtain it. A man reaps what he sows (Gal 6:7), so we must sow that quality in others if we are to reap it.

There must be some degree of competence, as well as loyalty, in those who are leaders. It is a hard thing to see a person who has been given a job on the basis of his loyalty and reliability struggling because he is unable to handle the responsibility. He may be utterly faithful, but is he able to manage his own home? He may really know his Bible, and his life may be consistent with its teaching, but is he able to convey that teaching?

The word that Paul uses for 'ability' in his letter to Timothy means sufficient, competent or qualified. He is not considering under this term natural or human qualifications. Elsewhere he writes of his qualifications and ability as coming not from himself or others but from God. His competence did not need any human recommendation, for it was self-evident in the lives which had been changed as a result of it.

It is often assumed that because a person is competent in the academic or business field, then that qualifies him for Christian work. An excellent teacher in school or college does not automatically have the same ability to inspire faith in the people of God. Similarly, people are often required to attain certain academic standards in order to prepare them for God's work. People still struggle for academic qualifications in order to enter denominational colleges, and one Christian organization I heard of only accepted workers who had gained a degree. Is this honestly synonymous with God's requirements? What are the qualifications that he is really after?

A servant heart

High on my checklist would come the quality of a
servant heart. In Old and New Testament times,
part of the apprentice's responsibility would be to
serve his teacher. Joshua was the servant of Moses
(Josh 1:1); the disciples served Jesus; Timothy
served Paul in many and varied ways, from bringing his cloak and parchment to him in prison (2
Tim 4:13) to the more rewarding work of visiting
and encouraging the Christians at Thessalonica in
Macedonia (Acts 19:22).

Jesus himself demonstrated the heart of a servant when he washed the feet of his disciples, setting them an example which he urged them to
follow (Jn 13:1-17). Furthermore, he taught that to
have a servant heart was a basic requirement for
anyone who was to be a leader in the kingdom (Mk
10:42-45).

I well remember my early days of serving the
Lord 'full time'. One of the first jobs I was given
to do was muck-spreading—good old farmyard
manure with a good old country smell! Hardly the
work, I thought, for someone who was called to
preach the gospel. But God said to me that if I was
not prepared to spread muck for his glory, then in
no way was I prepared to spread the word for his
glory.

I wish I could say that it then became easier and
more joyous, but I'm afraid that it didn't. Neither
did I see any decrease in the number of mundane
and humiliating things I was required to do.
Nevertheless, I did them. I guess I passed the test,

because I did graduate to spreading the word.

I remember that a young man, who was looking for an opening for ministry, came to stay at the community where we were living. He came out into the garden where I was doing some mundane task. The leader of our community gave him some old clothes and a pair of wellies so that he could join me and talk about 'ministry'.

I gathered from his expression that this was not quite what he'd expected, and from his attitude I felt that these sort of things must have been below his dignity. He stayed a few days and then left, obviously disillusioned with the whole scene. A number of years have passed and, sad to say, that same man is now a discredited minister. I cannot help wondering if the absence of a servant heart in those early days had something to do with his later problems.

Now a servant heart does not imply the kind of servility which is often thrust upon servants of God by the church, whereby the lives of ministers and Christian workers are characterized by the mark of being 'under'—underpaid, undervalued, under-estimated and under orders! This is not self-denial, this is being denied. We cannot deny ourselves something we do not first possess. Paul speaks of his right as a Christian worker to be supported by those to whom he ministered. This was a right, among others, that he was prepared to deny himself. It was his choice, and was not thrust upon him by a miserly diaconate or eldership.

Jesus showed the supreme example of a servant heart:

. . . who, being in very nature God, did not consider equality with God something to be grasped, but made himself nothing, taking the very nature of a servant (Phil 2:6-7).

Self-denial is simply what it says, choosing to deny self. It is not an emotional or spiritual black-mail by which others persuade me to deny my rights. Equally, if a person has always been a servant, it is not an act of self-denial for him to continue as a servant. He must first know what it means to be free and independent before he can deny himself and become a servant. I am thinking of the kind of person often found in Christian circles, whose life is characterized by serving. They willingly take on all the menial tasks which others thrust upon them, never complaining, never questioning.

I remember one such person, a young lady, who came to see me. On the surface her behaviour seemed so 'Christian', but as we talked another picture emerged. Because of her own lack of self-worth and the fact that she had never found a place where her interests were considered, she felt guilty if she thought of her own needs. She had hidden resentment and anger towards others who had exploited her willingness and servitude, regardless of her own feelings. She had to discover herself and her true value in God before she could really deny herself and serve others with dignity as an heir of God and joint-heir with Christ.

Beware of exploiters, the abusers of servants, those who use their power in emotional or spiritual blackmail to rob you of your selfhood. Jesus said about his own life, 'No-one takes it from me, but I lay it down of my accord' (Jn 10:18).

Have you noticed that with so many of us the difficulty lies not in being willing to serve but in allowing ourselves to be served. Some feel embarrassed or ill at ease when others seek to serve them. These people are characterized by self-giving service to others. I remember a time when I quite literally followed the example of Jesus. I took a bowl of water and a towel, and washed the feet of those who were in leadership with me. One elder at first refused. What I found interesting, and I believe significant, in his refusal was that he was a person exceptionally unstinting in his service to others. Happily, like the disciple Peter, he also changed his mind.

Let's consider for a moment this incident in the life of Peter (Jn 13:1-17). We are all familiar with the facts. Jesus, eating the passover meal with his disciples, takes a bowl of water and a towel and fulfils the duty of a menial servant as he washes their dusty feet. When he kneels before Peter, Peter is adamant, 'No, you shall never wash my feet.' Then comes this extraordinary statement from Jesus, 'Unless I wash you, you have no part with me.'

Consider what exactly Jesus is saying to Peter here. He was emphasizing that Peter's future with him did not depend on his willingness to serve, but first to be served. His ministry, gifts, leadership and all that he had to give would depend on whether he was willing to receive. I would go further by saying that we are only able to minister to the extent to which we allow others to minister to us. So many Christian leaders are busy ministering to others, yet are unable or unwilling to allow others to minister to them. It reminds me of the busy barber who was asked by a customer, 'Who cuts your hair?'

We need to recognize those who have a servant heart and a willingness to serve and be served, which leads me on to the next characteristic which I look for in an apprentice.

A teachable spirit

A willingness to be taught is one of the first indications that I look for as evidence of new birth in Christ. New-found joy or enthusiasm can be transitory, and the real fruit of a changed life develops gradually, but a teachable spirit, with a willingness to be instructed in the way of faith, is something that should be evident from the start. The word 'disciple' actually means 'learner', therefore a willingness to learn is vital for all disciples of Christ, particularly for potential leaders.

Teachableness is closely linked with meekness, a Christian virtue not to be confused with weakness. Meekness is a harnessed strength which can be understood by the illustration of a horse that has been trained and instructed to respond to the reins of its instructor. The term used to describe horses which have undergone this process is 'broken in'. I think this is unfortunate since it suggests that the strength and spirit have been smashed, which is not true. A properly-trained horse loses neither of these characteristics. Rather, both are harnessed and channelled in a way that can be utilized to best effect.

I sit writing this in my study where I have a picture on the wall, drawn for me by a young Christian French girl. The drawing is of a horse rearing up on its hind legs, but saddled, and with a bit and bridle, though significantly with no rider. 'You are like a wild horse,' I had told Christine, 'running free in whatever direction you feel so inclined, fearful of being controlled. You need the strength and enthusiasm which you have for Christ to be harnessed so that he is able to channel it.' A few days later Christine communicated to me the fact that she wanted to be teachable: I found the drawing on my desk with a quotation from Psalm 32:8-9:

> I will instruct you and teach you in the way you should go; I will counsel you and watch over you. Do not be like the horse or the mule, which have no understanding and must be controlled by bit and bridle or they will not come to you.

I told another young man I know that he was like a bucking bronco, and if I was asked to put a saddle on him I would be very wary because I stood the risk of being kicked to death. Unfortunately he is still 'running wild', quite unteachable.

Being teachable does not mean being unquestioning, stifling doubts and fears, or not challenging what is expected of us. Jesus did not expect such attitudes from his disciples. Some of their greatest learning times came out of honest questions (such as those recorded in Mark 10:20-27). Teachableness is an attitude of heart that says, 'I want to learn. I may question, I may challenge, I may even resist what is being taught, but in my heart I want to learn.'

Some will learn easily and readily, whereas others will put up resistance. The latter drain energy and patience from their teachers, but they must be encouraged, for they are learners. Beware of the 'apprentice' who is unwilling to learn, who believes that because he has the call of God on his life and the Spirit of God in his heart, he does not need to be taught. You will probably recognize this type of person because likely as not they will come to you and quote 1 John 2:27—'As for you, the anointing you received from him remains in you, and you do not need anyone to teach you.' Clearly the fact that this was true for John's readers did not prevent him teaching them more than the basic doctrine they already knew—even as 'little children' (3:18; 5:21; 2:18).

Another indication of teachableness is the way a person reacts to criticism or correction. Someone who reacts defensively puts up barriers, showing that they are entrenched in their position and unlikely to change. In that situation they are unteachable.

I remember one such person. Nothing that went wrong was ever his fault, someone else was always responsible. He felt threatened and became defensive towards any form of questioning, accountability or correction. I spent hours with him, and had him to stay in our home, but it was all to no avail, he was not teachable.

In contrast, I was recently handed a tape by a young apprentice. It was a recording of a talk he had given in his fellowship. He said to me, 'I want you to listen to this, and please let me know if you have any comments to make. I would be very grateful to hear them.' That is a teachable spirit. As the writer of Proverbs says,

> He who listens to a life-giving rebuke will be at home among the wise. He who ignores discipline despises himself, but whoever heeds correction gains understanding (Prov 15:31-32).

A person who is not corrected will not gain understanding.

There are various ways of correcting someone. One golden rule I endeavour to follow is never to correct someone in public. An apprentice who is making a hash of a meeting won't be helped by being corrected in front of everyone. Follow the example of Jesus and wait till it can be done in private, thus encouraging him to try again in the future (Mk 9:28). Public correction will also have the effect of discouraging observers from aspiring to public ministry in case they may be subjected to the same treatment.

Teachableness and how we react to correction takes me on to another aspect of apprenticeship—our attitude to authority.

Submission to authority

Much has been said in recent years about submission and authority. We can see from the story of Adam and Eve that our fallen human nature is resistant to authority, especially God's authority. It is important to recognize this, and to learn to respect and submit to authority. However, it has to be said that there has been a great deal of wrong teaching on this subject, and the whole authority/submission relationship has been carried to ridiculous extremes.

Firstly we must understand that submission to authority is not a club to beat people with in order to stifle any questions they may have. Neither is it intended to bolster up insecure leaders, nor to be used as a means of establishing control. Hebrews 13:17, which speaks of obeying leaders, was not written for leaders any more than Ephesians 5:22, 'Wives, submit to your husbands,' was written for husbands. They are not verses to be used as a demand for submission, but primarily for the direction of followers and wives.

Problems are created when a husband uses Ephesians 5:22 as a demand of his wife. She will counter by quoting verse 25: 'Husbands, love your wives.' We find ourselves majoring on what we consider to be our rights rather than on our responsibilities.

I was visited on one occasion by a young wife who was desperate about her marriage and what she felt her husband should be doing that he wasn't doing. I gave her a sheet of paper and told her to draw a line down the middle. I then asked her to make a list on the left-hand side of all she felt was entitled to her as her 'rights' within the marriage relationship. She gave me a wry smile and said that she'd need more paper. When she'd completed this list, I asked her to write in the right-hand column what she considered to be her responsibilities. This was a much shorter list.

When she'd finished I asked her which column she was living in. Without any hesitation she realized it was the first one. So I suggested that she went home and tried living in the second one for a month and see if she was any happier.

Happiness is not a goal, it's a consequence of living a life in which I fulfil my God-given responsibilities. We hear so much in our world about rights; women's rights, workers' rights, management rights, civil rights. But the Bible is more concerned with our responsibilities.

If someone is to be apprenticed they must have this healthy attitude to authority. Let us consider this more closely.

I suppose the classic example of someone who really understood the meaning of authority, and demonstrated it, is the centurion in Luke's gospel (Lk 7:1-10). Because he was a man under authority, he was able to recognize the authority of Jesus. I do not believe that anyone can be in a position to exercise authority until they know what it is to come under authority.

Within the church, the ultimate authority we come under is God's, but we also experience his authority delegated through others. Similarly, the centurion was not directly under Caesar, but the officer of a cohort who was responsible to the officer in charge of a legion which comprised ten cohorts. The chain of authority continued like this until it reached Caesar himself.

Authority comes from our position rather than our person. Any God-given authority which is mine to exercise comes from my position—in Christ, in the church, or in my family—and not from my person. However, my personality may be suited to my position, as was probable in the case of the centurion. It would be pointless giving a man the position of officer in the Roman army if he was undisciplined or unable to fight. Paul told Timothy of the qualities which should characterize a man who is to exercise authority in the church (1 Tim 3).

Failure to recognize that authority comes from our position rather than our person leads to two other wrong attitudes. The first of these is that respect for authority will only be given if the person deserves it rather than if his position deserves it. But this is not the attitude David showed to Saul (1 Sam 24:4-7), or Paul to the High Priest (Acts 23:1-5), neither of whom really deserved the respect or recognition of authority which they received. In the same way we should obey the command to honour your father and mother, irrespective of the sort of people they are. Respect is their due because of the position they have, not because they deserve it.

The second problem arises when people do not exercise their authority because they feel they do not deserve it. The fact that it is not deserved may well be true; nevertheless, it has been delegated to us by God, so it is right to exercise it. Demons do not recognize our worthiness, but our authority as children of God, and it is on that basis that they respond (Eph 6:11).

Imagine a policeman about to arrest a criminal 'in the name of the law' then hesitating and letting go because he feels unworthy of the authority which he has. If such attitudes prevailed in our country, we would end up in chaos. Some policemen would not be exercising authority because they would not believe themselves to be worthy enough to do so, while those that did would be totally oblivious to any faults they had. It would be rather like the situation in some of our churches.

Back to the centurion and Jesus. Have you noticed how a right attitude to, and recognition of authority are closely allied to faith? 'Say the word, and my servant will be healed,' the centurion said to Jesus. 'For I myself am a man under authority, with soldiers under me. I tell this one, "Go", and he goes; and that one, "Come", and he comes.' Jesus' comment on the centurion's attitude was that he had not found such great faith even in Israel. It is possible to recognize authority without having faith, but it becomes a heavy legalistic burden for us. It is impossible to have faith without recognizing authority.

I well remember my first painful introduction to this understanding. When we were first married, Hilary and I were part of a Christian community. The leader was a less experienced Christian than I was, and he often asked me to do things that I found difficult, or made decisions concerning the work with which I disagreed. My struggles over this situation finally came to a head. As I was arguing it all out with God, he challenged me one day to submit to those in authority over me. At that point I entered into one of those battles with God which I knew I couldn't win, but which I pursued with intensity until I could finally say, 'Right, Lord, I will submit to him and trust you in this situation. I am going to do whatever this man asks me and trust you with the consequences, so you had better make sure that by the time it gets to me it's what you want.'

Something important had happened. I had

learnt before to trust God directly, but now I was learning to trust him in a deeper way, to trust him through others. It was one of the most significant lessons I have ever learnt in my walk with God. Soon after I learnt this lesson, God began moving me out to exercise leadership.

One of our house-group leaders had been to a Bible week where he had been challenged to, 'Go back and submit to your leaders.' He was still struggling with this when he came to see me. He wanted to know if I would tell him in what direction I was leading the church so he could decide whether or not to submit to me. I told him I wouldn't.

Suppose I had told him and he was satisfied, but then in a few weeks' time we believed God wanted us to change direction or emphasis? What concerned me even more was that he was really saying, 'Philip, I do not really trust you, give me something else that I can trust.' This, as I pointed out to him, is the first step towards legalism, namely trusting in the letter rather than the person. Even more serious, I told him, was the fact that he wasn't trusting God. I illustrated my point by relating to him my experience at the Christian community. I am delighted to say that he also responded positively. We became very close friends, and it was a sadness to both of us when not long afterwards the Lord led him away from us out into a position of leadership in a new pioneer work.

A right attitude towards authority is important for all Christians, particularly for those being apprenticed with a view to leadership.

There may be times when we are asked to do irksome things, or things that seem irrational and pointless, or even things with which we disagree. I imagine this was probably how the disciples felt when Jesus spoke to the Samaritan woman (Jn 4:27). It is at this point that faith comes into operation. If we can trust God and the leader concerned, that is best; but if we can only trust God in the leader, then that is sufficient.

'Ah,' someone might say, 'must I always submit irrespective of what I am asked to do?' Of course not. When faced with an issue similar to the one that faced Peter and John, obey God rather than man (Acts 4:18-20). In my experience, however, these situations are exceptions that prove the rule, and our hearts should be inclined to submit to those in authority rather than resist.

A heart for God

There are a number of other characteristics we should look for in would-be apprentices, such as commitment to Christ, the development of Christian character, and the evidence of spirituality. All of these and most of the characteristics that I have already mentioned, with the exception of 'calling', are different aspects of one essential quality that I would call 'having a heart for God'.

This quality was certainly true of the original Twelve, or at least the Eleven. With all their imperfections, of which there were many, the one distinctive virtue they had in common was their devotion to Jesus and their desire for the kingdom. They were enthusiasts, prepared to leave family and job in pursuit of something they believed in. It is true that at times they were impetuous, or fired with personal ambition and, on occasions, quarrelsome.

Nevertheless, their hearts were on fire for God which meant they were open to being changed by him into strong leaders of the church.

I believe that, given time, leaders can be developed from those who are 'called' and who have 'a heart for God'. I do not find it difficult to cope with and even forgive the over-exuberance of such people if their desire is to know God better and serve him with all the energy they can muster. Mistakes made by these enthusiasts can usually be rectified, exuberance can be tempered with growing maturity, and desires and energies channelled.

In a parable concerning the kingdom of God Jesus spoke about how a seed of corn is planted and how it grows in a certain way—first the stalk, then the ear, and finally the full kernel in the ear (Mk 4:26-29). Farmers, like Christian leaders, want the full, mature fruit. But unlike some Christian leaders, farmers know that a certain process has to take place before the fruit is apparent, let alone mature. The seed is planted, and for some time there is nothing to be seen. Then the stalk comes, often in a rapid surge of growth, but there is still no inkling of fruit.

When there is a surge of activity, perhaps among young people, or in the 'charismatic' churches, people question, 'Where's the fruit?' Give it time. Yes, first the stalk, then the ear, and only then the full kernel. That is the order, despite our desire to reverse it. Our duty is to be patient until maturity comes, rather than to dismiss people prematurely.

In my early days as Director of British Youth for Christ, I introduced a system of Associate Evangelists. The reason I did this was simple. As I looked at those who were being used as evangelists in the country, I realized that many of them, when young and inexperienced, had received their grounding with the National Young Life Campaign. At that time it seemed that NYLC were no longer doing this, nor was I aware of any other organization prepared to take the risk of training young, inexperienced, potential evangelists, and giving them opportunities to develop their ministry. In the future there would be a lack of the mature ministries which churches and Christian organizations would need. So I started BYFC Associate Evangelists to meet this need and to provide a training ground for young evangelists.

I termed these evangelists 'associates' because we could not afford to pay them. I prayed for ten and got ten. They were relatively untried, some untrained and with little experience, but each had a sense of God's calling and a real heart for him. This was sufficient for us to let them loose on the unsuspecting youth of Britain. I used to say that it was like trying to get a bunch of carriage-horses pulling in the same direction with very few reins to control them.

The fact that BYFC did trundle along speedily, albeit rockily, was good. But more important is that the original objective of the scheme has been reached. Those inexperienced and untried young men are now leaders on the national scene.

Having a heart for God is something I find difficult to describe but relatively easy to recognize. Jesus spoke about it in his words to the Christians at Ephesus who had so much to commend them in terms of perseverance, holiness and orthodoxy, yet had forsaken their first and chief love, and consequently faced the risk of having their work closed down (Rev 2:1-7).

Have you ever heard of a couple with a heart for each other who find it difficult to find time to be alone together, or need to be told that they ought to. More often the problem is keeping them apart. Again, imagine saying to a young lady in love, 'Why don't you tell your friends about him?' No, the difficulty is usually shutting her up!

How does this relate to serving? I remember a wife handing her husband a pair of his shoes which she had beautifully cleaned for him. 'Surely you don't clean your husband's shoes!' was the horrified remark of another man's wife. 'I would never do that for my husband.'

'I don't do it because I have to, I do it because I love him,' she said simply. This couple loved one another so deeply that it was no problem to serve each other, however humble the task. In the same way, there should be no real difficulty for those who have a heart for God, and have made Jesus their first love, to spend time with him, talk about him, or gladly serve him. By contrast, you will find that attempting to motivate, develop and channel the potential of those who basically have no real heart for God is a time-consuming and fruitless task.

7

Nurturing

Let's assume that a group of budding apprentices has been found, and I am satisfied that they have the potential to be developed. But where do I go from here?

First, a relationship with each individual must be established. It is then essential for that relationship to be nurtured. I have discovered that it is one thing to initiate a relationship but quite another to nurture it. Failure to do so may mean that a relationship that began with much promise will wither and die through frustration, disappointment and finally disillusionment.

Paul gave time and care to nurturing—relationships between his apostolic team and various churches they had planted. Writing to the Thessalonians, he said,

> We were gentle among you, like a mother caring for her little children. . . . We dealt with each of you as a father deals with his own children, encouraging, comforting, and urging you to live lives worthy of God (1

Thess 2:7, 12).

Surely there is no more powerful example of nurturing than that of parents nurturing their children. We shall come back to this passage in due course, but first let us look at the example of Jesus.

Mark 3:13-15 describes how Jesus initiated a relationship with the twelve. He

> went up into the hills and called to him those he wanted, and they came to him. He appointed twelve —designating them apostles—that they might be with him and that he might send them out to preach.

The phrase 'that they might be with him' is rather like a piece of meat between two slices of bread. Jesus called the twelve, but before he could send them out into powerful ministry their relationship with him had to be nurtured. The key in their development as leaders was the nature of the relationship which was built between master and disciple.

Even though it may be argued that their initial call and designation was of a functional nature, it became very evident in the following months that the relationship which Jesus had with his disciples was a deeply personal one. They were not just designated preachers or leaders, they were friends of Jesus.

Did Jesus enjoy being with his disciples on occasions other than when he was ministering to them or with them? Did he value their friendship and their company? I believe it is very clear that he did. It is a sad fact that in a great many leadership situations today, relationships seldom get beyond the functional level. The prayer of Jesus was that the disciples should be one, just as he was in the Father, and the Father in him (Jn 17:21). Their relationship with him should be like the relationship that exists in the Godhead.

But what exactly is the nature of this relationship in the Godhead? Purely functional? If that were so, how did they relate to one another before creation? Was it a distant relationship? Did they have anything in common? Or could it be said that they enjoyed each other's company, found total fulfilment in it, and did not actually need anyone or anything to complete it? Surely this last is the truth of the matter.

I remember a young man asking my advice about which group of believers he should join. He was caught in a conflict of loyalties. Should he join the group whose hierarchical structure he was in agreement with, or should he join another? Having prayed about it, he was still no clearer. I advised him to go where he had real relationships. He was still not sure how to assess this, so in order to make the point clear I told him to go with the ones whose leaders he would go on holiday with. He quickly made a decision then.

My point was that people normally go on holiday with those they have chosen, not with those they feel obliged to select. Holiday-time is 'off-duty' time, and I have discovered that to ask myself how I would like to go on holiday with certain people gives me a quick and accurate assessment of my relationship with them.

Thank God we are beginning to recover and appreciate not only the value of personal relationships, but also the necessity of them within the churches. I say recover, because it is very clear from looking at the early church that their life was community based, and that worship and witness flowed out from their normal interaction with other believers (Acts 2:44-47). The church grew rapidly, and was able to proclaim good news because it *was* good news in itself.

In times past when we were mainly a rural society, worship was an extension of relationships which already existed. The church building was in the centre of the village and that was where the local community met together on Sundays for worship.

The Industrial Revolution, which accelerated the transition to an urban society, changed all that. People who came to worship together were individuals with little or no interaction with one another during the week. Slowly there developed what has been called 'billiard-ball Christianity'—people who clicked together on Sundays, then returned to their separate pockets.

The characteristic of our British reserve encouraged the individualistic emphasis on worship, which then became confused with spirituality. But the greater interaction a person had with God, the shallower their interaction became with other people. So church worship became a gathering of individuals cocooned in their own silent aura, with the briefest acknowledgements of each other's presence—a smile, a nod, or a whispered 'hello'—before drawing the veil tight. For the really spiritual it was best to avoid all eye contact, preferably by closing the eyes. Pleasantries might be permitted afterwards.

If we are to develop relationships on a personal level, then we'll need to spend time together on occasions other than functional with those concerned. Let me hasten to add that I do not believe we should operate simply on the basis of choosing to build relationships just with the people we happen to like. The disciples were not given the option of choosing their master or choosing each other.

At the heart of our Christian relationships there must be a sense of God joining us together, otherwise our relationships will be painful and lacking in substance. A child was heard to sing in our church, 'Grind us together with cords that cannot be broken.' The effectiveness of our witness is determined by the quality of our relationships. Jesus said, 'All men will know that you are my disciples if you love one another' (Jn 13:35).

Encouragement

If I had the opportunity of being a parent all over again, I would give much more attention to encouraging my children. Being an encourager has not come naturally to me; I did not experience much encouragement when I was growing up. My parents never actually discouraged me or prevented me from doing what I wanted to do in life. On the contrary, once I had come to a decision they backed me in it. What I felt I missed was their encouragement when I was formulating my decision.

We all need and respond to encouragement. The Holy Spirit is the great encourager. He is not only there helping us to make the right decision, but he is also alongside us, encouraging us in the outworking of that decision.

There are times when we feel like Elijah, afraid and depressed; we've had enough and are totally exhausted (1 Kings 19:3-5). It is at such times that we need encouragement, and God saw to it that Elijah received just what he needed. It came in the form of an angel bringing food, water and rest—isn't that just like God? When Elijah was at a pinnacle of faith, God ministered to him by ravens (1 Kings 17:2-6), but when he was in the pit of despair, God sent an angel (1 Kings 19:5-9). Our natural inclination would probably be to reverse the order, but God—being a God of encouragement—knows when angels are needed.

When I first felt the call of God upon my life, I met very few who actually encouraged me. There were many who advocated 'playing safe'. Others were anxious to point out the dangerous pitfalls, while yet more people gave me good reasons why I should not step out in faith. Very few told me to risk all for God.

But what I wanted to do more than anything else was to risk all for God. I reasoned that I would rather go bankrupt for God than for anyone else. In my opinion he was the only one worth it. I decided that I would rather stand before God and say, 'I tried because I wanted to serve you,' than to hear him say to me, 'Why didn't you at least try?'

I thank God for men like Denis Clark. As a young convert I got to know him during a crusade in south-east London. He was my hero. When I preached my first sermon in a small country chapel, a month or two after my conversion, it was announced in the crusade office (much to my embarrassment). Denis showed great interest and talked with me about my experience, asking how many people had been in the congregation. When I told him it had only been about twelve, he commented that that was twice the number present at his first sermon. What an encouragement to know that this man of God, who preached to thousands, had started like that. I knew there were possibilities for me.

It was because of the encouragement I received from men like Denis, and the discouragement from so many others, that I vowed to God that I would seek to encourage others into the service and ministry of God. Some people may argue that it should surely be enough to have the Lord's encouragement; after all, David encouraged himself in the Lord (1 Sam 30:6). True, but that was because no one around him was prepared to encourage him—in fact they were on the point of stoning him to death.

The gift of encouragement (yes it is a gift) is desperately needed in the church (Rom 12:8). We need people who are called by the Spirit to get alongside others, encouraging them to go on, saying, 'You can do it, keep going.'

I remember going to watch one of my friends run in the London Marathon. As he appeared after running twenty-three miles, his face drawn and his lungs heaving, he needed all the encouragement he could get to finish the course. So intent was his wife on encouraging him, as she ran alongside him urging him on, that she ran slap-bang into a lamppost. There must be a lesson there somewhere about running risks to encourage others.

Go and encourage others. 'Run' alongside them. Tell them if you have seen them make progress, and tell them you appreciate what they are doing for God.

Giving thanks

'I thank my God every time I remember you' (Phil 1:3).

Paul not only let God know that he was grateful for the Christians at Philippi, he also let them know in his letter to them. We are often so slow to show our appreciation of one another. We seem to think that if we show others that we appreciate them we might run the risk of 'robbing God of the glory', or that we might cause them to become proud. I believe that the real reason we fail to show appreciation is in order to protect ourselves.

When we really do appreciate something we become that much more caring about it, and more responsible for its safety. Let's just think of some things we appreciate—maybe a car, or a job, or a gift we've received. Surely we value them and care for them that much more because we appreciate them. Exactly the same applies to people whom we appreciate. Once we begin to show our appreciation we are committed to caring for them.

Jesus was not slow to show his appreciation. In his letters to the churches in Asia, wherever there was anything to appreciate or commend, he did so unhesitatingly (Rev 2 and 3). He showed his appreciation first, not in order to soften the blow of criticism, but simply because he saw and commended good first.

It is a sad fact that we do not give voice to our appreciation. I know this is true of me. Hilary has cooked many, many good meals for which I have not voiced my appreciation, but if she makes a mistake with one, then I always comment. I hope I am learning to rectify this. I hope we are learning in our churches. People should not be allowed to work without words of appreciation. It should not happen that the only time comments are made is when things don't go right. We are all encouraged when we are shown appreciation, and motivated to go on and do more for God.

Personally I find it a great encouragement when people show their appreciation of my ministry. In recent years I have had to get used to people clapping my sermons, and I have to confess I enjoy it. I don't think it's because my sermons have improved that much, but rather that the people I preach to are more prepared to express their appreciation.

Sometimes in our small groups and teams we have had times of speaking out our appreciation for those things that we recognize in one another for which we can truly give thanks to God. We mention those qualities and gifts of God that we see expressed in each other's lives. The value of this in terms of building people up in God cannot be realized until it has been experienced.

We should not have to wait for specially planned meetings in order to speak out our appreciation. Rather, like Paul, we should declare, 'How can we thank God enough for you in return for all the joy we have in the presence of God because of you?' (1 Thess 3:9).

How many people know that we give thanks to God for them?

Caring

Nurturing could be summed up in this one word.

Caring for others in a meaningful and effective way was surely what Paul was referring to when he wrote:

> We were gentle among you, like a mother caring for her little children. We loved you so much that we were delighted to share with you not only the gospel of God but our lives as well, because you had become so dear to us. . . . For you know that we dealt with each of you as a father deals with his own children, encouraging, comforting and urging you to live lives worthy of God, who calls you into his kingdom and glory (1 Thess 2:7-8; 11-12).

Do we show Paul's concern for the growth of others? Do we care enough that we will work night and day so as not to be a burden to them? Do we care enough to share our lives with them as well as the gospel? Do we care enough to confront them when this is needed? I remember saying to a friend that if necessary I would risk my friendship with him in my concern for his well-being. The depth of my care for him would be proved by my willingness to stand back and let God deal with him.

I can think of times when those whom I have been training have gone through deep trials. Everything within me has wanted to step in and shield or rescue them, only to hear God saying to me, 'Don't you dare go near them—I am doing my work.'

'But God, they will think I don't care,' I would reply. In return, God would say, 'Afterwards they will know that you have cared more for them than you care for what they may think about you.'

Nurturing is caring for others—enough to see them succeed in God's way.

8

Women in Ministry and Leadership

I believe the issue of women in ministry and leadership is going to be a big one in the next few years. There has been a significant change from 'one-man ministry' to 'body-life ministry' which has brought into focus the fact that women, being part of the body, are therefore included in its ministry. As one man said to me, 'I used to interpret ministry as "pulpit ministry" only, but now that I see it as body ministry I have changed my views on the right of women to minister.'

I have no doubt that in the near future we will see more and more women emerging with ministries and leadership gifts and being accepted by the majority of churches. If this is so, it is as important to prepare women through apprenticeship as it is men.

For the past eight years I have been working closely with women in ministry and leadership teams. Initially I was a member of such a team; later I went on to share the leadership of another one with a woman. During that time I must have studied every possible scripture on the subject, read a number of books, and listened to most of the arguments for and against women in leadership. Taking all this into account, and recognizing the anointing and blessing of these women, I am fully satisfied that women do have a valid part to play in leadership in the church.

As I have said, I have heard most of the arguments against women in leadership. A popular one is that Jesus had only men in his team. True, but he also had only Jews. Does this mean that the future leadership of the church must lie in the hands of Jewish men? The fact is that it was not appropriate at that time for Jesus to have either women or Gentiles as part of his apostolic team. But by excluding them, he was not setting a pattern for all time.

Jesus was quite prepared to break down some of the established religious and social barriers regarding women. He had women travelling with him (Lk 8:1-3). He was quite prepared to talk in public with a woman, even a Samaritan one (Jn 4:9). He surprised his disciples by this contact, and was misunderstood by them and others when he was prepared to receive ministry from women (Mt 26:6-13). Few people have been more highly commended for their service than Mary was in her act of extravagant love.

I believe that God must grieve when he sees so many potential gifts and ministries—in fact, well over half the church—locked up in what a friend of mine calls 'frozen assets'.

Paul also highly valued the ministry and friendship of women in his work. He writes of women who contended at his side (Phil 4:3). He links them in the same sentence with men as 'fellow workers', and by that I don't think he meant doing secretarial work or making drinks after the fellowship meetings!

Romans 16 shows how highly Paul respected women and their ministry in the church. He writes of Phoebe, a deacon in the church. (The word he uses here for deacon is used elsewhere to refer to himself and other male leaders.) He declares that she has been a great help to many, including himself. In the next verse Priscilla receives commendation along with her husband, Aquila, both Paul's fellow-workers, and in verse six Mary, who has worked hard for the church.

In verse seven we have the intriguing question of Junia (or is it Junias?) who is commended along with Andronicus as being outstanding among the apostles. The former spelling is the feminine version of Junianus, the latter a masculine version of the same name. Certainly some early leaders in the church considered that this apostle was in fact a woman. Chrysostom, one of the early bishops much respected by the Reformers, writes, 'Oh how great is the devotion of this woman, that she should be counted worthy of the appellation of apostle.'

A little further on in the same chapter Tryphena and Tryphosa are commended for working hard in the Lord, and Persis is described as a dear friend of Paul's. Other women are also singled out for greeting, and although nothing is said about their ministry, the very fact that they are mentioned shows that Paul did not move in a male-orientated Christian society where women played little part in either the ministry or social life of the church. The whole tenor of Paul's writing seems to indicate that women, as well as men, played an active part in the life of the churches he visited.

I am not naïve enough to assume that I can change anyone's mind on the subject of women in ministry with the brief treatment given here. I am concerned that so often there is more heat than light generated when this subject is raised and in no way do I wish to fuel the fire. We must, however, be aware of the enormous inconsistencies that the church has lived with for many generations. We have sent women off with our blessing to minister on the overseas mission field, yet denied them the right or opportunity to minister at home.

I have known men who object to women in leadership, but then tell me of the blessing they have received from women who have ministered to them. Conversely, there are men who publicly speak of the right of women to be part of an apostolic team, but have only men in theirs. These attitudes often result in men struggling to perform a ministry for which they are neither suited nor anointed, while there are women in the church who are obviously gifted and would be ministering were it not for the fact that they are women.

I am fully aware of all the different views on this issue, the scriptures that are used to support them, and the dangers that each view highlights. It reminds me of the arguments I used to hear, as Director of BYFC in the seventies, concerning Christian rock music. In the end I came to the conclusion that what was really a cultural or emotional issue, or simply a matter of taste, had become 'the-ologized' and thus open to being categorized as 'right' or 'wrong'.

I believe that we should be including apprentices in our leadership teams, and this includes women as well as men. I would apply the same test for suitability for apprenticeship to a woman as I would to a man. Is she called? Has she a servant heart? Is she teachable, faithful and able? And does she have a heart for God?

I would probably add one further question to this test: is the situation appropriate for women in ministry and leadership? This would be applicable if the team was working in a culture which did not allow men and women to mix in public, or for women to play a leading role in society. These are situations which surely do not apply to us in the UK where, at the time of writing, both our head of state and head of government are women. Another example of inappropriateness would be where the team would consist mainly of women led by a man, especially if he was a single man.

Having said this, I am convinced that there are many occasions and opportunities when it is both right and appropriate for women to be included in apprenticeship in order to develop their gifts and ministries so that they can take their place in the leadership of the church.

9

Apprenticing by Example

Teaching by example is the most natural form of teaching there is. We learn as children from our older brothers and sisters, for good or for ill. We emulate our father or mother. 'Don't put your elbows on the table,' my mother used to tell me as a child. 'But Mum, Dad does it.'

'When you're as big as your father, you can too,' was my mother's refuge. I can still recall my satisfaction, when I was finally as big as my father, in deliberately putting my elbows on the table and smiling defiantly at my mother.

How many times have you heard a person giving his testimony say something like, 'I realized that a friend of mine had something I didn't have, and I wanted it.' That friend was simply being an example.

Of course, one can give a bad as well as a good example. It was Friedrich Nietzsche, the atheist philosopher and founder member of the 'God-is-dead' theology, who, having stayed with a Christian family when a student, is reputed to have said, 'If they had acted more redeemed, maybe I would have believed in their redeemer.'

Leaders are people who set an example which others choose to follow. Those who follow them do so because they have confidence in them, and believe that they will lead them into good things. Paul, recognizing the influence a leader can have, instructs Timothy: 'Set an example for the believers in speech, in life, in love, in faith and in purity' (1 Tim 4:12).

The church as a whole should be an example to the world. One of my favourite verses about the church is Ephesians 3:10, where Paul reveals the intention of God 'that now, through the church, the manifold [literally: multi-coloured] wisdom of God should be made known to the rulers and authorities in the heavenly realms'. Isn't that amazing? Just as raindrops display the full range of the colours of the rainbow when a beam of sunlight shines through them, so the church displays the full range of the wisdom of God to the heavenly rulers and authorities. We are that church, and we are that example.

Look and learn

By far the most effective way of teaching is to demonstrate first, giving an example for others to follow, and then to watch them do it, giving encouragement and suggesting necessary improvements. This method is at the heart of making apprentices.

My recent experiences at golf demonstrate the effectiveness of this way of teaching. Having seen professional golfers on television making the game seem so easy, and since I'd been hacking around for months, I decided to have some lessons. To say it was a revelation would be an understatement. Having an expert right alongside me, demonstrating, watching, helping me to make adjustments and showing me what I was doing wrong, was an illuminating experience. I would like to be able to say that my golf has improved dramatically, but it's too early to tell yet. As I told my curate friend and playing partner, 'I now know what I'm doing wrong, and at least I'm able to fail with style, but I'm learning.'

When Jesus wanted to give his disciples a lesson on learning, he took a towel and a basin of water and washed their feet. He then went on to say, 'I have set you an example' (Jn 13:15). Someone has aptly said, 'An ounce of example is worth a pound of exhortation.'

In the same way Paul sought to train the church at Corinth. They had no heritage of Christian experience, no New Testament scriptures, no devotional books or autobiographies of the great saints. What model could they choose on which to base their Christian life? 'Follow my example,' Paul advised them, 'as I follow the example of Christ' (1 Cor 11:1). Again, writing to the church at Philippi he said, 'Whatever you have learned or received or heard from me, or seen in me—put into practice. And the God of peace will be with you' (Phil 4:9). And to the church at Thessalonica he wrote, 'You became imitators of us and of the Lord. . . . And so you became a model to all the believers in Macedonia and Achaia' (1 Thess 1:6-7).

I have heard many Christians say, 'Don't look at me, look at Jesus.' Although they may sound pious and humble, what they are actually saying is 'I am so aware of my inadequacies that I do not really believe you will see Jesus in me, and because I want you to see Jesus, please don't look too closely at me.'

Of course, saying that we are an example in no way implies that we have reached a state of perfection, or that we are infallible. Just look at some of the great leaders throughout the Bible—Moses, Elijah, Samuel, David, Peter, Paul. They are portrayed honestly, with all their faults and foibles as well as their strengths. They are men 'just like us' (Jas 5:17). Their weaknesses did not prevent God from using them as examples for others to follow.

God intends to display now his multifarious wisdom through the church. He is not waiting for us to reach perfection, but wants us to take a look at ourselves, and see that we have something to show people right now. As I told my local fellowship, we haven't got it all, we certainly do not have enough, but we have got something of God through which we can show others how to follow Christ.

When the disciples saw Jesus at prayer they wanted to emulate him. 'Teach us to pray,' was their immediate response (Lk 11:1). This reminds me of an occasion when a pastor of a church in Eastern Europe asked me to go with him and pray for a sick member of his congregation. This same pastor had previously spoken to me of his concern that so few men in his church were equipped to take responsibility. I refused to go on the visit with him, and instead told him, 'Take with you a man from your congregation, let him see you pray for the sick person, teach him to follow your example. Then next time send him with another.'

I have already said that in my early Christian life Denis Clark was my hero. He was also my example. I learnt how to pray from listening to Denis pray. When he prayed I could sense the gates of hell rattling on their hinges. He assaulted the forces of darkness in the name of Jesus.

In those early days I discovered that I had even learnt to speak like Denis. He was South African, and I just couldn't figure out why people thought I came from South Africa until it dawned on me that I had patterned my life on Denis to even this degree. His love and respect for the word of God, and his evangelistic heart and ministry, were all good examples which I sought to emulate. I think the only area in which I did not follow his pattern was in his sermon construction, and those who knew Denis will know that this defied imitation.

But surely patterning one's life on someone else is dangerous? Wouldn't it have been better just to pattern it on Jesus? It could have been dangerous for me to emulate Denis had he not been so completely committed to Jesus and to seeking to follow his example. For me who knew so little about Jesus, it was helpful to have a living example of what it meant to live for him and like him.

Let's consider in greater depth how we can be an example for others to follow.

The theory

It is essential that before we even begin to set or

follow an example, we know what it is we are seeking to develop, and the principles by which it may be achieved.

I find it significant that although Paul writes to a church about a particular problem, his letters usually begin with a statement of doctrine before he goes on to write about the practical outworkings of that doctrine. The inference is clear—we are not going to live in a right way until we believe what is right, for what a person really believes about God will determine the way he behaves. As A. W. Tozer says in his excellent little book *The Knowledge of the Holy* (James Clarke 1961):

> A right conception of God is basic not only to systematic theology but to practical Christian living as well. It is to worship what the foundation is to the temple; where it is inadequate or out of plumb the whole structure must sooner or later collapse. I believe there is scarcely an error in doctrine or a failure in applying Christian ethics that cannot be traced finally to imperfect and ignoble thoughts about God.

There is almost an unspoken objection to the subject of the doctrine of God in these days, and if not an objection then often a disturbing ignorance. The attitude of so many seems to be, 'Let's not bother with the theory, let's get down to the practice.' Maybe it's a reaction to the overemphasis on theory without the concomitant practice that we have known in the past, but nevertheless, we shall not be able to produce the right result consistently unless we understand the theory behind it.

The practice

Once we have explained to people about the quality of life we are trying to achieve, then we should demonstrate this quality in our own lives. The supreme example of this is God demonstrating his character in the person of Jesus. Men of God had long known about the glory of the Lord. Some, like Moses, had longed to see it (Ex 33:18). But it was in Jesus that God revealed his glory. As John writes,

> The Word became flesh and lived for a while among us. We have seen his glory, the glory of the one and only Son, who came from the Father, full of grace and truth (Jn 1:14).

As Christians sharing in the nature of God, we can also demonstrate his love and power. Paul writes to the elders at Ephesus, 'You know how I lived the whole time I was with you' (Acts 20:18). To his young apprentice Timothy he writes,

> You, however, know all about my teaching, my way of life, my purpose, faith, patience, love, endurance, persecutions, sufferings—what kinds of things happened to me (2 Tim 3:10).

I guess some of us would have to confess that we could only say, 'You know all about my teaching.'

Timothy was able to experience the demonstration of God's nature in Paul by travelling and working with him. Just think how much potential leaders would learn if they could be around older, more experienced men of God. If they were able to be there when they prayed, visited the sick, counselled others and preached. It cannot be done? It can. It is possible even in a counselling situation. Those being counselled will often welcome the opportunity of sharing and praying with more than one person.

Getting close

It is difficult to show how something is done without allowing people close enough to see. This can present its own problems. Supposing people get close enough to see our inadequacies and failures? Supposing they see that we are nearly all talk and very little practice; that we preach eloquent sermons on prayer but do not pray ourselves? Perhaps they will discover that I get irritable and impatient.

Yes, they will probably discover all this and a lot more besides. It simply means that we will have to be very honest, which is not a bad thing for all concerned.

I must say that for me it was a delightful surprise to watch Ian Andrews minister healing. He encouraged people to gather round and watch what happened, asking some if they would like to try, correcting them if they did it wrongly, sharing in their obvious delight when God healed.

I can imagine the early disciples learning from Jesus in the same way. I can imagine Timothy saying to himself, 'Oh, is that how it's done? I could do that.' Perhaps he even thought he could do better than Paul and, who knows, maybe he did with a bit of practice. I must confess that a lot of my ex-apprentices are doing things much better than I ever did—and I am proud of them.

No carbon copies

When I was Director of British Youth for Christ we held an annual Easter conference. At one conference we were encouraging people to be creative, and I took a small group to experiment on making a cartoon. I had trained originally as an artist and had some experience in cartoons, so I thought it would be fun to make a point through humour.

The outcome of our creative effort was a large cartoon of a converting machine. Being fed into one end of the machine was a vast number of young people of all shapes and sizes and styles of clothes. As they went through the machine, various hammers knocked them into shape and a reject valve let out those who wouldn't be shaped. Then there was an ejection tube that blew out things considered to be unsuitable, and slots to feed in the right diet. All of this was controlled by a machine operator, and finally, at the end of the machine, out came a long paper chain of identical people who were carbon copies of the operator. 'Every church should have one' was the title we gave to it.

It caused a bit of a smile at the time, but nearly all humour has an element of truth in it, even though it may be very exaggerated.

'Isn't your child like you?'

'Oh, do you really think so? I hadn't noticed really.'

Of course we had noticed, and secretly hoped others would recognize it too. This is perfectly understandable and for the most part harmless. The harm comes when we do not respect a person's own identity and individuality and try to make them a copy of ourselves.

'Let us make disciples in our own image' has too often been the guiding principle in the church. If we are going to make apprentices, we must accept that every person is unique and allow for that fact. Each one will be different and will not necessarily think as we do or have the same gifts. Even if they do, they may not approach them in the same way.

I remember trying to help one apprentice in his sermon preparation. After more than a little frustration on both our parts, I realized what I was doing. I was assuming that he had the same thought processes as myself and therefore would approach the whole matter in the way I would. As a matter of fact he didn't and still doesn't. I had been getting frustrated with this person because I thought that to prepare his sermon properly it had to be done my way. My way was obviously 'the best' because it worked—for me. But it was not a question of best or worst, simply different. It was a lesson which I trust I learned well. There must be no carbon copies in the making of apprentices. Each person is unique, gifted by God, and must be respected for his individuality.

Taking risks

To my mind one of the main causes of failure to develop people and their gifts and ministries is the unwillingness of leaders to take risks. Leaders want to be sure that a person really does have a gift and a ministry from God. They look for a degree of expertise or experience that will ensure the blessing of God before the person is given opportunity to minister. The reasons for this are simple—leaders do not want to take either the responsibility or the risks involved. Sometimes it is both.

There are a lot of frustrated young people in our society today. They apply for a job only to be told at the interview that the company is looking for someone with experience. How the young person is supposed to get experience without someone first giving him a job is both a mystery and a source of frustration to him.

Equally, there are a lot of frustrated people in our churches. 'You have to be a superstar before you can get on in our church,' was the remark made by one such person in a growing church. Their remark is probably an exaggeration born out of frustration, but it does highlight the problem of how a person can develop from inexperience to an experienced ministry without someone giving them an opportunity to try. Giving them such opportunities undoubtedly involves taking risks.

When I was Director of British Youth for Christ, I took on an inexperienced young man as an associate evangelist of BYFC. No one else would take him on, and I knew I was taking a risk in doing so (see Clive's own remarks at the front of this book). The fact that this young man, Clive Calver, eventually succeeded me and became an outstanding Director of BYFC, before going on to be General Secretary of the Evangelical Alliance, has shown that it was a risk well worth taking.

Although some of the risks I have taken in this area have been successful, others unfortunately have not. But of this I am sure—no one will be successful in developing craftsmen from apprentices if they are unwilling to take risks. It is possible that some apprentices will develop into outstanding craftsmen. It is equally possible that you could choose someone who gets it all wrong and lets you and himself down very badly.

If this happens you will be in good company. Jesus had twelve apprentices; Judas turned out badly, and Peter blew it on more than one occasion before becoming an outstanding leader in the church. We need to remind ourselves that both were specifically chosen by Jesus in the same manner as all the others. As we have seen, Paul had his successes and failures: Timothy was a success; John Mark, for a time, an apparent failure (Acts 13:13); Demas, another of Paul's team, turned away, finding the world too attractive (2 Tim 4:10).

The difficulty of taking risks

I have found it difficult to take risks when it is so much easier to do things myself, especially when I know that I can produce a more acceptable result. I remember when my sons were younger and one of them would struggle to make a model aeroplane. I would watch as the glue spread around, affixing itself to everything in sight. Gluey fingers, gluey hair, gluey clothes and gluey furniture, but a relatively small amount where it was supposed to be.

Frustration would build up in me and my son as I manfully resisted the temptation to take over. I believed I could do it more quickly and more efficiently, and that the finished article would look like the picture on the box. I would struggle inwardly, 'Is he going to botch it up completely? Is he going to be so frustrated and humiliated by criticism that he will be put off model-making for life?'

However important becoming a successful model-maker may be, the risks involved are minimal compared with the risks we take in training apprentices for ministry. I remember only too vividly being involved in the early days with a schools' ministry, visiting schools and speaking in Religious Education lessons. Gordon Bailey and I were pioneering in this field, and we came to a very simple agreement. Gordon would cover the top half of the country and I would cover the bottom half.

Even with my lack of ability in arithmetic, I could work out that in planning to visit each school twice a year I would be severely limited in the number of schools I could visit. So I decided that I needed some apprentices who could regularly be with me on my school visits. I would travel to a school with one of these young men and they would watch me at work for a day or two. They would question and learn, then midway through the week would come their big opportunity—their first class. By then I had usually worked out which class—if any—was the most placid, but it was still a nerve-racking experience for both of us.

Part of my difficulty was an internal one—my own insecurity which brought about an anxiety if I was not in control. That is something I have had to deal with if and when it comes to the fore. The other part of the difficulty was knowing that so much was at stake. I don't mean whether or not I would be allowed back into the school if the lessons became a riot. No, it was something much more

serious than that. We were dealing with eternal
issues, matters of life and death. Quite literally, this
might be the only time that the young people in
this class would hear the truth about Jesus. Alternatively their future openness to the gospel could
be determined by how well the apprentice handled
this perceptive and critical group. With so much at
stake, was it worth taking the risk when I knew I
could handle the situation better than they could?

Many is the time that I have sat on my hands,
buttoned my lip, squirmed inwardly and prayed
desperately as the apprentice struggled with a class.
Was it worth it? On the whole it was, but some of
the best craftsmen in this field don't know to this
day the agonies that I went through on those
occasions.

Risks must be taken if people are to develop their
ministry. What we must do is to allow them to take
risks in situations where the damage done, if they
make a hash of it, will not be too great either to
them or to others. Learner drivers don't go on
motorways. The risk involved is too high. It is ex-
pecting too much of a learner driver to cope with
such a responsibility, and the damage they might
do is too great.

I learned to drive when I was thirteen years old.
We lived on a huge estate with miles of private
tracks and roads, and we had an old US army jeep
in which my father taught me to drive. Even
though the risks were reduced, I still found my first
drive a daunting experience, especially when at the
end I drove into the garage, panicked, and
smashed the bike of my father's assistant against
the garage wall. Distraught, I retired to my room,

but my father soon had me down again, back in the jeep and driving in and out of the garage until I could do it with total confidence. Incidentally, my father also paid for a new bike for his assistant.

Let's not expose those with a developing ministry to a position which could really destroy them if they failed. I shudder at times when I see young men and women thrust out to lead a church of people in the most vulnerable and difficult of circumstances, and those which would tax the ability of the most able and experienced leaders. It is sad to see people with such promising ministries retire disillusioned and humiliated into relative obscurity.

Is it worth it?

Why take the risk when so much is at stake? The answer is quite simple. We should because God has done so.

Have we ever stopped to consider the enormous risks that God has taken? Think for a moment. Who of us in launching a new enterprise would choose as its leaders men who just six weeks previously had deserted and disowned us? Which of us would select as chief spokesman on our behalf someone who had denied all knowledge of us at our hour of trial? I'm sure none of us would take such a risk.

What about us? It seems as though God has staked his honour in his future church and his programme for world evangelism in the likes of us. What a risk! And it's not as if God couldn't have done better. He has deliberately chosen the foolish, the weak, the lowly and the despised, to accomplish his purpose (1 Cor 1:27-28). It is not a matter of 'Poor God, look who he's stuck with. It's a shame there are not more able, powerful and influential people in the church so that much more could have been accomplished.' Not at all. God could have chosen the cream of this world, but instead he chose people like you and me.

Isn't that a terrible risk? Doesn't God know what we are like? How can he entrust us with such responsibility? Or does he know something we have forgotten? The answer, of course, is that God is not blind to our faults, and he does not trust us on our own. What he has done is to put someone in the church whom he can trust totally—the Holy Spirit. If God so trusts the Spirit in us, can we not do the same with others? Is that not an acceptable risk for us to take?

The fact that I can trust the Holy Spirit in others has undoubtedly been one of the greatest factors in my taking risks with people. This is not a matter of wishful thinking or sheer presumption; that would be tempting God. It is that place of faith where I can sense that God is telling me that I can trust him in that person and let go.

At such times the risk has proved to be immensely rewarding. I cannot begin to tell the enormous pleasure it has been for me over the years to see young men and women stretch and grow as they have responded to the trust that I have put in them.

Making steps

If people are to develop in their gifts and ministries

they will need to be provided with steps whereby they can rise in accordance with their experience and ability.

Let me explain what I mean by making steps. When I became Director of BYFC there were two full-time workers in the whole of the movement. This was not just because of a lack of money to employ others, but more because of a lack of opportunity.

I felt that BYFC had become a stop-over place where keen young Christians could gain experience in youth evangelism before moving on to some other area to give their lives in the service of God. Just when these young people were gaining experience and ability, BYFC lost them because there were no opportunities for them to make progress within the movement. These people had to go elsewhere just when BYFC could have gained most from their increasing effectiveness. I decided to make steps within the structure of the organization so that those who wanted to develop gifts and ministries would have opportunity to do so without having to leave.

I have seen the same sort of difficulty within churches. Ministries and gifts have been lost to the church simply because there is not the opportunity to develop and make progress within the local fellowship. I can never understand why churches do not provide a series of steps within their own structures so that people are able to develop their gifts and ministries to the highest possible level.

When I moved to Guildford to work alongside David Pawson we sought to grapple with this problem. The gap between pew and pulpit was a big one—too big for people to make the leap. What could be done to encourage ministries to develop? Close the gap by lowering the standard of ministry? That was obviously not going to help in the long term. Import ministries at the highest level? As I have said earlier, the problem with that option is that it does nothing to develop the people already in the pews.

Again, I believed the answer was to create steps to give people the opportunities they needed to enable them to rise, according to their ability and gift, to the highest possible level of ministry. As a result of this, the church took the unprecedented step of selecting a young man from among the membership and giving me the responsibility of apprenticing him. The fact that he later became a full member of the ministry team, and now leads his own team in another church of some 250 people, proves the wisdom of creating steps.

If churches do not provide such steps they will face two dilemmas. The first is that people will have to develop their ministry elsewhere. For some this will be right because of a clear leading from God, but for others it will be born out of frustration. The second dilemma is that gifts and ministries will stay undeveloped because people will stay where they feel comfortable and relatively safe.

Stirring the nest

> . . . like an eagle that stirs up its nest and hovers over its young, that spreads its wings to catch them and carries them on its pinions. The Lord alone led him . . . (Deut 32:11).

Apparently the eagle has to encourage its young to fly. It will hover over its young, giving them a demonstration. If the young still refuse to leave the security of the nest, then the parent eagle will begin to dismantle the nest twig by twig. If that doesn't produce the desired effect, then the eagle will carry its young high in the air and drop them, forcing them to fly but always being close at hand to catch them on its wings if danger threatens.

Drastic action maybe, and rather unnerving for the young eagle, but if it is ever going to learn to fly, let alone learn to soar into the heavens, then some steps have to be taken to encourage it to stretch its wings and launch out.

Most of us probably feel a certain amount of sympathy, if not identification, with the young eagles. We like to stay where we feel safe and comfortable, however high up the cliff-face it might be. We like to stay within the limits of what we know and have learned to depend on, rather than launch out into flights of faith.

A few years ago I experienced just how easy it is to rely on external props. For years I had taught that the church was people, not buildings or programmes. 'Church is what's left when the building falls down,' as someone has observed. I had believed that with all my heart, but I did not realize how much I had come to depend upon external props until we found ourselves with a church which had neither a building nor a programme. My little nest was stirred up rather drastically, and once more I found myself having to find my security in the living God.

If we are going to encourage people to grow and

develop themselves and their ministry, then we may have to begin to dismantle a few nests—those comfortable little places that people have settled in. Could Abraham ever have become the father of faith if he had remained in the comfort and security of Ur? I doubt it.

Recognizing obvious potential in one young lady, I sought to encourage her to use her gifts more. Her immediate response was, 'Oh, I leave that to my husband.'

'Why, what are you afraid of?' I asked her.

Her immediate and very honest reply was, 'Failure.' Her fear of failure was keeping her in a comparatively safe and comfortable place, when she could have been launching out to fly and soar in the same way as her husband.

Dr Paul Tournier in his book *A Place for You* (SCM Press 1968) says of Adam after the fall, 'His hiding place among the trees was not his place, but an alibi.' An alibi or a nest, it can amount to the same thing—some place to stay where we feel more comfortable and secure.

I believe that many in our churches have opted for the safe and secure rather than the flight of faith. Undoubtedly God has called many to serve him in Sunday schools and youth departments and as deacons, but just as assuredly, many have settled there because that is where they feel comfortable and secure. I praise God for men like John Wimber who stir the nest, challenging the church of God to launch out and soar upward on the wind of the Spirit.

When should people be encouraged to move out and move on? Well, if the analogy of the eagle and its young is anything to go by, it would be just before they feel able and ready to move. Be warned though. However necessary it may be to stir a nest or two, do not be surprised if it produces a lot of squawking and flying feathers in the process. I cannot imagine that the young eagles are terribly happy about the disturbance to their domicile.

10

Space Invaders—or Creators?

As apprentices become more and more skilled, pressure inevitably begins to mount over finding space in which to use these skills.

Preaching has been almost the sole responsibility of the 'master craftsman', but apprentices are now becoming more skilled in the art of preaching and teaching. Opportunities will have to be made and space created if tensions and frustrations are to be avoided. The same applies to other responsibilities involved in leadership.

As apprentices become more proficient, they will be more able to take responsibility for greater tasks and to exercise authority to make responsible decisions. They may well come to perform these tasks as efficiently, if not more efficiently, than the one who has trained them. This is the time when the trainer will need to create space for those ministries to develop.

Removing the cork

As room at the top becomes more crowded, something has to happen. The pressure will mount, and unless the leader plans ahead and takes the initiative, he will become like a cork in a bottle. Wine experts tell us that corks are extremely necessary if wine is to reach its full maturity; they only become a problem if they stick in their situation for too long. Like a connoisseur of wine, a good leader will know when the time has come to 'pull the cork'. He should always be prepared to work himself out of a job.

Playing the power game

The alternative, of course, is that as apprentices mature and become increasingly proficient, the leader feels increasingly threatened. He feels that his space is being invaded by these up-and-coming ministries, and this can spell danger for all concerned. This is the time when people start to play their power games.

The quest for, and the clinging to power is not confined to the political arena, nor the boardrooms and shop-floors. The power game and the struggle for the lion's share of authority is contested just as fiercely within church circles. I must confess there have been times when God has convicted me of playing it as selfishly as others, and there have been other times when I have been the victim of a power struggle.

King Saul is a classic example of what can happen when space at the top becomes a little cramped

(1 Sam 18). He more than any other was responsible for recognizing the potential in David. It was Saul who warmed to David, took him into his service and made him an armour-bearer (1 Sam 16:21-22). David's brothers showed nothing but scorn for him in his willingness to fight Goliath (1 Sam 17). It was left to Saul to recognize David's faith and bravery. It was Saul who personally commissioned David and sent him to fight Goliath.

Let's not forget the risk that Saul took. If David had failed, all Israel would have become subjects of the Philistines (1 Sam 17:8-9). I suspect that few of us would be willing to place our position, our families and our own future into the hands of an untried youth. Saul's interest in David did not stop at his victory over Goliath. David was taken into Saul's house and given promotion as he continued to succeed in the tasks he was set. It seemed the basis of a good relationship.

So where did it begin to go wrong? The turning point was God's rejection of Saul as the King (1 Sam 15:26), and Samuel's anointing of David (1 Sam 16:13). Trouble started coming to the surface as David's prowess began to compete with, and indeed exceed, that of King Saul. 'Saul has slain his thousands, and David his tens of thousands' sang the delighted people of Israel (1 Sam 18:7).

Perhaps the people were insensitive in exalting David above the King. Maybe Saul should have accepted the reality of the situation with good grace. But if we're honest, I believe many of us would admit to feeling hurt and having twinges of jealousy if we suddenly found that the one we had apprenticed was now receiving greater acclaim than ourselves.

We might not resort to the open hostility that Saul showed when he felt threatened and insecure, nor hurl spears at people, trying to pin them to the wall. Yet I suspect that much of the veiled criticism directed against people and their ministries within the church is often an attempt to destroy the threat that we feel they pose to our own security.

When an invasion of space is threatened for those at the top—even if unintended—this can sometimes bring devastating results in leadership and disastrous consequences for the people. When the Magi visited King Herod they asked him of the whereabouts of the one born to be King of the Jews. This was immediately perceived by Herod as a threat to his position and he plotted to remove that threat—with dire consequences for the young boys in Bethlehem.

King Saul's fear and jealousy of David affected the life of the whole nation. Resources of manpower that could have been directed against the enemy of Israel were wasted on either pursuing or being pursued in internal conflict. Loyalties became divided as people took sides, and it was years before the people were united again and Israel recovered her former glory.

Paul reminds us:

> These things happened to them as examples and were written down as warnings for us, on whom the fulfilment of the ages has come. So, if you think you are standing firm, be careful that you don't fall (1 Cor 10:11-12).

How, then, can we avoid such calamities?

The need for sensitivity

Although the people of Israel were accurate in their assessment of David's prowess, they were hardly sensitive in their expression of it. Singing the praises of David was one thing, but drawing comparisons with Saul at the same time was somewhat thoughtless.

One can sympathize with a new leader who is constantly being compared (usually less favourably) with the one he has succeeded, but what about the leader who has been succeeded and is now being told how marvellous his successor is? Or what about the minister who is being told what a great preacher his curate or assistant is? These judgements may be true, but they can be given with a remarkable lack of sensitivity. Of course such leaders should be secure enough in God and in their calling not to be hurt or jealous. Nevertheless, if people really do care for their leaders they should be sensitive to their feelings.

Those who are called to succeed should also show a fair measure of consideration if they are to avoid problems. I must confess to feeling a degree of sympathy with the brothers of Joseph (Gen 37), although I do not condone their actions. Let's face it, when Joseph, the second youngest son, was favoured by his father above all his brothers, that was hard enough. Then he was given the heir's robe, against all known tradition, in preference to his elder brother, which made it even more difficult for them. But then as a seventeen-year-old he had the audacity to tell his brothers, not once but twice, of dreams he had had which predicted that he would rule over them and they would submit to him. Who could not feel sympathy for them? Joseph may have been right in all he said, but he was unwise and insensitive.

By contrast, though I have some sympathy for Saul because of the people's insensitivity towards him, I have the greatest admiration for David. In the long years that David was pursued by Saul, never once did he refer to his own anointing and his rightful calling to the throne of Israel. Not once did he get involved in a power struggle with Saul. He had many struggles, as his psalms reveal, yet David's struggles were not with Saul but with God.

Saul or Jonathan?

If we are to avoid wrong attitudes and disastrous reactions we would do well to learn from a comparison of Saul and Jonathan. Both their futures were threatened by David, but each showed a very different attitude.

What was this difference in attitudes? Quite simply, Saul was motivated by power and Jonathan was motivated by love.

The hunger for power and the desire to control and dominate others is a basic instinct within the human heart. It was the instinct to which Satan found a response in Eve's heart in the Garden of Eden: 'For God knows that when you eat of it your eyes will be opened, and you will be like God' (Gen 3:5). To be like God was to have access to power and the ability and authority to exercise it.

It was this same hunger which Jesus found displayed in his disciples. James and John asked Jesus for position, favour and power, to sit on either side of him in glory (Mk 10:35-45). The indignation shown by the others could, I suppose, have been righteous indignation at the audacity of James and John. But Jesus' remarks to them all imply that the indignation sprang from their own desires for power and position.

Whatever their motivation, Jesus was at pains to point out that the desire to dominate, control and manipulate others is not the way of the kingdom of God. God's way is loving and serving others.

The choice before us is quite simple, either we succumb to our desire for power and control, or we follow the way of loving and serving. We cannot do both, and the more we seek to do one, so our desire and ability to do the other will diminish.

We can see this principle at work in the relationship between Saul and David. As Saul sought to dominate and control David, so his love for David, and incidentally for God, diminished. His attitude of deep respect and trust quickly changed to outright hatred and hostility.

Jonathan, on the other hand, was motivated by love for David (1 Sam 18:1-4). It was not just that Jonathan recognized the anointing of God upon David's life, there was more to it than that. Cynics might argue that he was motivated by self-preservation. Knowing that ultimately David would succeed to the throne, he was preserving his family's future for that eventuality (1 Sam 20:14-15). If that was the case he was running an enormous risk, because in supporting David he put his own life at stake with his father Saul (1 Sam 20:33).

No, Jonathan's love and his covenant relationship with David meant that he would at all times seek David's good and protect him, even at the risk of his own life. It meant that he was willing for David to succeed to the throne, even though he realized it meant that he would never sit in that position of power. Few people ever reach this point of sacrifice. It is true that many show no aspirations to power but that is because they have no access to it. We can only truly sacrifice what we first possess.

Their relationship, however, was not one-sided. The moving story of Mephibosheth shows that David was just as committed to Jonathan as Jonathan was to him (2 Sam 9).

When space becomes cramped, someone may have to step aside to make more room, and this requires very special relationships, such as that between David and Jonathan.

David's or Solomon's temple?

The lessons we may learn from David are not confined to his succession to power. We may also learn from his handing over of power (1 Chron 28-29).

David's great desire was to build a temple for God. God denied him the fulfilment of this desire and told him that his son Solomon would build it instead (1 Chron 17). To his credit David did not go away and sulk or become jealous, but rather he did all that he could in order to help Solomon succeed in the task.

The vision to build the temple was David's. He was the one who poured out his heart in prayer, the one who assembled the plans, who exhorted the people to give and who himself gave quantities of precious metals and stones. It was David who appointed 'stone-cutters, masons and carpenters, as well as skilled men in every kind of work' (1 Chron 22:15). David appointed priests, overseers, musicians, singers, gatekeepers and treasurers—and yet we still call it Solomon's temple.

I wonder if David minds? I wonder if he is sulking in some corner of eternity, bitter because after all his efforts someone else has received most of the credit? I don't think for one minute that he is. David was a leader who created space for others, and I'm sure he was more interested in the temple being built for God than whose name it was remembered by.

There is, however, an even greater example than David or Jonathan. It could be argued that Jonathan gave up the right to become king because he recognized that God had anointed another to reign. One could say that David gave up his intention to build the temple because he was denied the right to build.

What about the One who was King of Glory, who was anointed to reign and had every right to that position? He had access to unlimited power to which he was never denied the right; but he voluntarily gave it all up, made himself nothing, took the very nature of a slave, was made in human likeness and came to serve fallen humanity. He was the One who carried his obedience so far that it took him to the most degrading and painful death that man could devise. Why did he deny himself so much? It was in order that we might succeed, that we might become children of God, heirs of God and joint-heirs with Christ himself (Rom 8:17).

'Your attitude should be the same as that of Christ Jesus' Paul tells the Philippians (Phil 2:5).

As a young Christian, when I became aware of the call of God upon my life, I was challenged by the story of David and his willingness to work and let someone else get the credit. In my youthful enthusiasm I immediately told God that I was prepared to follow the example of David, but I must confess that it has not been easy, and at times it has gone very much against the grain.

I am sure I am not alone when I say that I like to receive recognition for what I have done. God certainly recognizes that we all have that need, and he has every intention of responding to it. Why else would he give the promise of reward at the day of Christ (1 Cor 3:14)? Which one of us has not been motivated to serve by the thought that one day we may hear those words, 'Well done, my good servant' (Lk 19:17)?

My encouragement is that, whoever has been responsible in building his temple, the Lord will give his own recognition at the day of Christ. In the meantime I have to have the same attitude of mind as Jesus himself, and that means denying self and making space for others to succeed.

11

Letting Go

It is as true for every Christian leader as it is for every parent that there comes a time when we have to let go of those we have reared.

During their growing phase the young in faith have been steered through the difficult years of immaturity. Their knowledge of God has deepened, their leadership skills developed, and having arrived at some real measure of Christian maturity they are now ready and able to exercise responsibility in the kingdom of God. By this stage their maturity should be recognized, as should their readiness to be released into ministry.

But when exactly is this point reached, and how important is it for people to be released in this way? Paul writes about the importance of releasing people into responsibility in his letter to the Galatians, though in another context.

> What I am saying is that as long as the heir is a child, he is no different from a slave, although he owns the whole estate. He is subject to guardians and trustees

until the time set by his father (Gal 4:1-2).

A Jewish child could possess a great deal of wealth which could not be released until he was recognized as an adult person. For the Jewish boy there was a fixed time when he was recognized as an adult. When he reached the age of twelve he was taken into the synagogue and he became a 'Bar mitzvah' or 'Son of the Law'. The father prayed, 'Blessed be thou, O God, who has taken from me the responsibility for this boy.' The son then prayed and in his prayer acknowledged that he was now responsible for his actions before God. There was, and still is, a clear dividing line in Jewish society between boyhood and manhood.

The Greek boy was in his father's care from the age of seven to eighteen. He then came under the care of the state for two years. Again, there was a clear line of demarcation between boyhood and manhood.

For the Roman boy the age was not fixed, but between the ages of fourteen and seventeen a festival would take place when it was clearly recognized that the son had now arrived at manhood. However, although a Roman son was recognized as a responsible adult, he was never released from his father's authority. By law the father had absolute authority over his family. This would continue when his son married, and extend to his grandchildren. He could sell his son into slavery and even had the right to execute him. The son could attain to the highest office in the land, but his father was still in absolute control. The history of the 'godfather' goes back a long, long way in

Italian society.

In our own society no such clear dividing lines exist between childhood and adulthood. According to the latest ruling of law the contraceptive pill can be prescribed without parental consent to a girl under sixteen. Young people may leave school at sixteen and go out and earn their own living. At the same age they are permitted to ride a small motorcycle, become a voluntary patient in a mental hospital, consent to sexual intercourse, and get married with their parents' agreement. They have to wait a further year to drive a car or buy fire-arms. They have to wait yet another year to be served with alcohol, vote, take out a mortgage, make a bet or rule as king. When they reach the ripe old age of twenty-one they are allowed to be hypnotized in public! It is all very confusing. Just when do we consider that children become responsible as adults?

The issue may be even more confusing in the church. Forget for a moment the minefield that waits to blow up the unwary church leader over whether children should be allowed to take communion, or at what age as believers they can be baptized or become church members. An even bigger minefield is the question of the age at which a person reaches spiritual maturity when he or she can be considered responsible enough to come into leadership.

The answer depends very much on the circumstances we are in. Paul and Barnabas could appoint elders within the period of their first missionary tour which lasted only three years. From convert to church leader in three years! In some of our churches it takes as long as that to convince the leaders that we are ready to be baptized!

Age, whether in physical years or in the time one has been a Christian, has little to do with Christian maturity. There are those young in years, and relatively young in faith, who show remarkable maturity. The average age of the group which they may be leading can also have a bearing on whether someone is mature enough to lead. A predominantly youthful church can be led by correspondingly youthful leaders. As a friend of mine remarked of one such youthful fellowship, 'Someone is considered eligible for eldership when they are old enough to shave!'

In the Bible there are no clear rules of demarcation given to enable us to determine when a person is ready to be released into leadership. When it comes down to making such decisions, recognizing maturity is left to the judgement and discretion of the incumbent leader or leaders. These leaders may come anywhere between two extremes. There are those who may recognize maturity in others but release them too little or too reluctantly, and there are those who recognize this same maturity but release people too easily and give them too much responsibility.

Letting go too much

Some leaders operate on what might be called the Roman paternal system. Others more cynical than myself might call such leaders 'godfathers'. In this situation there is no question as to who has the authority, and that authority is retained throughout the relationship. Any release from this authority is usually only cosmetic.

Firstly, I must confess that I have a strong aversion to this kind of authority, and I do not find it scripturally justifiable, although some apparently do. Secondly, even discounting many of the horror stories which have been attributed to the 'discipling movement' (most of which seem to be either fictitious or exaggerated), I still find that there are attitudes towards the exercising and retention of authority which disturb me.

Did Paul, like a Roman father, always retain authority over Timothy whom he considered to be his son? It is difficult to reach that conclusion from reading the letters he wrote to Timothy. He writes as a father to a son, but as a father who appeals or urges from the basis of a love-relationship and esteem rather than one of authority and control.

Paul's letters to the churches which he fathered are also very revealing. In matters that concerned moral or doctrinal error in the church, his appeal is to their maturity rather than his authority. Even when his ministry, personality or integrity are questioned, Paul still writes, 'By the meekness and gentleness of Christ, I appeal to you' (2 Cor 10:1). The phrase 'I appeal to you' ('I beseech you' AV) is frequently used by Paul when he wanted some response from the churches. No doubt Paul's appeal carried some weight, and no doubt they would think long and hard before they decided whether to respond or not. Nevertheless, it was for them to choose.

Terry Brewer is someone whom I apprenticed for a number of years. Two years ago I handed over to him the leadership of the church. I had gradually created more and more space for him and given him greater responsibility until I believed it was right that I should step aside and give him the leadership of the church.

I was asked then, and am still often asked, about the nature of my present relationship to that church. I would say that it's like that of a father to a son who has grown up and got married. You do not stop being a father, but you do stop having responsibility in the new relationship.

Doesn't this create difficulties and dangers? Yes it does, and it has. You may end up losing everything. You may well have to come to terms with feelings of being no longer wanted. You may experience tensions and questions about how, in practical terms, the relationship will work out.

There may be many difficulties to work through and, like Paul in his relationship to churches, I have not been exempt from these. However, I have found that working through the difficulties produced by letting go is infinitely preferable to hanging on.

When to let go

In handing over authority I tend to work to the following principles.

Firstly I consider whether the people concerned are able to take responsibility for the task. Not that they are able to do as well as I think I can do, or handle the job without making mistakes, but are they able to shoulder the responsibility, whatever form it may take?

Secondly, I have to ask myself whether I am ensuring that they have sufficient authority to fulfil that responsibility. Have you noticed how often in church circles a person is asked to fulfil a responsibility without the authority to do so? Leaders are often expected to take responsibility while being hindered from doing so because the necessary authority lies elsewhere, maybe with the church meeting, or even with an outside body. This creates an almost impossible situation for the leaders as they have no authority to make meaningful decisions.

Thirdly I consider whether the authority is nearest the point of action. In a battle situation it is obviously preferable that decisions, and authority for those decisions, are made nearest to where the action is taking place. It would be ludicrous if a commander on the field had to refer for a decision to open fire to someone far removed from the battle. Politically decisions can be made elsewhere, but decisions regarding action need to be made by the one who is in charge and on the front line.

In most organizations decision-making tends to rise higher and higher up the organizational structure and thus further and further away from where it matters. The results of this are delayed decisions, out-of-touch leaders and frustrated people. Good leaders will avoid this situation by allowing the authority and decision-making process to function nearer the point of action.

I am currently involved with a number of fairly new churches who have given me the responsibility and authority to set up firm leadership as a base for their work. How long will this relationship function, and will I always have the same degree of

authority? My answer is that when my job has been
completed, and an eldership or leadership is recognized, then I would let go. In doing so, my authori-
tative relationship would change as the responsibility is transferred to others. That does not mean
that my relationship with them ceases to exist, but it
does mean that functionally it operates on a new
basis.

Having said this, however, my friend and colleague John Noble tells me that I give things away
too readily. What does he mean by this?

Giving away too much too quickly

I have already written of my admiration for David,
particularly his ability to resist striving for the authority which was his by right, but which for a long
time was in the hands of Saul. The reason he did
not strive was quite simply that he still saw Saul as
the Lord's anointed one, established on the throne
of Israel. David was quite prepared to wait in the
wings until it was his turn to take centre stage.

What I do find hard to understand is the ease
with which David could step aside and abdicate his
God-given authority when his son Absalom rose up
against him (2 Sam 15). I am convinced that the
relationship which David had with Absalom was
based more on sentiment than reality. David quite
plainly failed to understand the intentions of his
son. Although rebellion by a son was punishable by
death, and God had made the parents responsible
for bringing his actions to judgement, it is quite
plain that David was unwilling to confront his
scheming son.

We can only conjecture why David failed to do this. Was he simply blind to Absalom's schemes? Was he unwilling to confront his son because of his own past guilt and failure concerning Bathsheba? Was David, like so many of us in leadership, guilty of neglecting his own family because of the affairs of the kingdom? Whatever the reason, we know that David took the easy road out and backed away from confrontation. I suppose it could be argued that he did it in order to protect others, but it would appear that his first thought was to protect himself (2 Sam 15:14).

It is easy to see how we can give away too much too quickly, rather than avoid painful confrontation. Fearful of the consequences both to ourselves and to others, it is a great temptation to back away. But this is not the only reason that we may be tempted to withdraw.

All the privilege, but none of the responsibility

My three children have grown up now. Two are married and one engaged to be married. Hilary tells me that I am becoming broody for grandchildren. I am certainly looking forward to that stage. I have talked to various friends who have become grandparents and they have convinced me that it's a great experience. One friend, however, did express the shock he felt when he realized that, amongst all the joys, he was married to a grandmother!

It seems wonderfully blissful to enjoy all the privileges of having young children, yet none of the responsibilities. As one grandad put it, 'You

can hand them back at the end of the day.' Who
wants interrupted nights and a house festooned
with drying nappies? Who wants their clothes
stained and smelling from deposits left by babies'
burps?

Yes, to enjoy all the privileges of a position without any of the responsibilities is blissful indeed. I
must confess that I did feel a little bit like this when
I handed over the leadership of BYFC to Clive
Calver. Now, I thought, I shall be able to enjoy all
the privileges while Clive takes the responsibility.
In actual fact, my thoughts reflected an internal
weakness: a desire to avoid the responsibility which
in itself could lead to my giving away too much too
early. (I would hasten to add that this was not the
case with Clive.)

Delighting in the success of those we will apprentice should be the heart's desire of all who aspire to
be leaders. Someone has said that the greatest thrill
is to lead someone to Christ. I would say that for
me there is a greater thrill, it is to see someone I
have led to Christ lead others to him. It has been a
rare privilege for me to enjoy the success of those I
have apprenticed. To really know this delight and
privilege we must be willing to recognize maturity
in these apprentices and to release them at the
right time and in the right way into the ministry
prepared for them.

APPENDIX

On the Other Side

by
Terry Brewer

The whole concept of discipleship was clarified for me not long ago when Phil took me to a golf club with the idea of teaching me how to play. My previous experience amounted to games of crazy golf or games with my kids on a local putting-course.

Most of our time was spent showing me how to hold the club, how to stand and how to swing. I thought it would be easier than it actually was. I had seen famous names on TV thwacking the ball effortlessly straight for the hole, and it all seemed fairly attainable. For me the reality was somewhat different.

The first part of my 'apprenticeship' to the game of golf was to watch Phil. He showed me how to hold the club, achieve the right line through the body and so on. Then it was my turn to practise holding the club. As I did so Phil made corrections, observations and encouragements. Then it was moving that club, aiming at the non-existent ball which in fact was a strategically-placed piece of rubber.

First I watched Phil do it, observing all his movements, remembering what he said, listening to his summary. My turn then came. As we progressed I seemed to have more and more to remember, and I kept going through it all in my mind. Phil continued to make comments as we went from stage to stage.

Our next move was to bring everything together. An actual ball was placed on the grass. Again I observed first, watching every move, remembering all the comments. Thwack! Off shot the ball, straight and true, finally coming to rest at about the 200 yard mark.

Then came the big moment—my turn. Holding the club, getting that swing right, connecting with the ball. Up went the arms, full stretch, go! Down came the club, arms straight, muscles straining, bags of concentration . . . crunch—the ball dribbled off the green and landed a few feet out onto the range. I tried again, and kept on trying until I got it right.

For me, being an apprentice has very much resembled learning to play golf. There has been much to learn, and many attempts to do things correctly and well; many mistakes, upsets, headaches and heartaches; a great deal of stumbling from one thing to the next before at last getting somewhere. In retrospect, the one thing that helped me more than any other to survive and succeed in apprenticeship was my willingness to learn. That may sound pretty straightforward, but in reality I was to find that the word 'willingness' covered virtually every area of my life.

Finding the right person to learn from

It was in the mid 1970s that I first felt I wanted to be what I believe is misleadingly described as 'full time' for God. At the time I remember saying to friends that I believed it was what God wanted for me. I think I felt that no one, not even the elders of the church, would listen or think it very important if I said it was what *I* wanted. As time went on it became increasingly apparent that it was also what the Lord wanted. The two need to go hand in hand.

This particular call seemed to evaporate as far as the church leadership was concerned after our initial discussions together. At that time, however, they were talking to Phil Vogel about his becoming part of the leadership team. As I was responsible for the youth work in the church, I was asked to chat to Phil about what we were doing with our young people. I found him to be someone I could talk to, and he also shared my heart for reaching out and seeing the church mobilized.

I was about twenty-nine years of age when I first met Phil. I owned my own home, I had a wife and three children and was succeeding well in my job. To come into a relationship and environment where I had to start learning dented my pride.

As an interior-designer and furnisher I had spent seven years learning my trade, and I breathed an enormous sigh of relief when it came to an end in my mid twenties. I was glad to see the back of all that studying, the endless lectures, seminars, demonstrations, courses and various examinations. The thought of going back into it all again depressed me. But inside I knew there was no other way. I had to be prepared to learn, to start from scratch.

I suppose this is best highlighted in the situation in which I found myself towards the end of 1977. I took unpaid leave from work and journeyed with Phil to York to be involved with him in some evangelistic and schools work.

Each night of this week of outreach there was a coffee bar with various activities taking place, all designed to bring in non-Christians. During the day we were in the various schools surrounding the York area.

I had never done schools work before. Phil and I had only talked about it, with Phil sharing his own personal experiences. The thought of standing up on my own and trying to communicate the Christian gospel in a relevant way to a classroom full of kids filled me with dread. Although I was involved in youth work, I discovered that explaining the good news about Jesus to a hostile class of the same age group was not the same thing at all.

As we went through the assemblies, special lunch-time meetings and lessons, I listened, praying quietly in tongues, while Phil was speaking. I sat back, prepared to learn and drink in everything that I could. I made sure that Phil didn't leave his briefcase anywhere, I made sure that he always had a cup of coffee when he needed it—to me nothing was too menial in order to gain valuable experience.

After a few days in the classroom, Phil turned to me and told me that I was to take the next lesson. I felt awful—completely inadequate and totally unprepared. I dreaded the very thought of it, let alone the reality.

I stumbled and staggered my way through the lesson, scribbling some drawing on the blackboard which was all supposed to show that God was a creator and that we needed to acknowledge that the world was made by a creator. I was gradually running out of ideas. In the end Phil stepped in and took over from me.

I felt terrible, an utter failure. I was sure I had ruined the gospel for that particular class. I wanted to run away and hide. I decided that this was not my calling. I was a square peg in a round hole. None of this was for me. What happened next, however, showed me that if my heart was willing then God was prepared to take me on.

After that lesson Phil, a singer who had accompanied us, and I all went to the staffroom for coffee. A few of us were chatting together when there was a knock on the door and a crowd of pupils outside asked to speak to me and the singer. They wanted to discuss with me what I had said. As a result of that particular lesson, an additional meeting was put on at lunch-time for me and one other person to explain the gospel in greater depth. I was so encouraged, and it was from that point that I

began to learn the lesson that it's not just down to me—
God likes to get involved as well!

If I had not been willing, I do not think that I could
have become an apprentice when the opportunity was
given. Nor do I think I could have stuck with it when the
going was so tough. To persevere as an apprentice was
difficult for me because by nature I was a rebel. I earned
that name at school, developed that reputation when I
came to the Lord Jesus, and caused real difficulties in
my first church because of it. When Phil first met me in
the mid-1970s he observed that the conspicuous chip on
my shoulder was an obstacle to growth.

I suppose the most significant factor in the shaping of
my life at that time was the fact that Phil took an active
interest in me. He watched what I did in the life of the
church and then questioned me about it. I would listen
to him for hours as he shared his experiences and all
God had taught him through them.

As we talked over a period of time, I discovered that
Phil had experience in the areas in which I wanted to
learn. He was also willing to give this knowledge away
and to take some responsibility for the consequences.
Through our relationship and time together I was making myself available to be apprenticed. Little did I know
that it was to take all my time and energy, physically,
mentally and emotionally.

I am not sure that either of us made a conscious decision, but somewhere along the line we committed ourselves to each other. Phil agreed to take me up and take
me on, and I agreed to listen, learn and put into
practice.

At that time I felt that Phil was the man to teach me,
but looking back on it now I am not so sure if there were
any other options open to me. No one else in the church
took on apprentices. They were all either (apparently)
too busy, or they didn't see any need for it (surely Bible
colleges were for training leaders?), or didn't know what

to do or how to go about it. That included the whole leadership in a church of some 500 people.

Apprenticing in practice

I had never been apprenticed before, and even then I didn't know that that was what we were doing. It's only looking back on it now that I can see the pattern clearly.

I had already begun to speak in small churches, chapels and Christian unions at schools and colleges whenever I was available and work permitted. I was also leading, with others, the youth work in the church. I was doing as much as my spare time would allow. I had to learn how to channel and use my energies for maximum effectiveness.

The relationship of teacher and apprentice between Phil and myself meant that I was accountable to him, so I checked things out with him and kept him informed about work I was doing and my life in general. As I learned to share my life, with all its longings and weaknesses, I realized that my failures did not disqualify me from the Lord's love or from continuing to take responsibility in those areas he had entrusted to me.

Phil and I would discuss everything I did. I remember my first sermon in the church, to a congregation of some 500 people—not exactly small beginnings! I spoke for forty-five minutes and someone came to the Lord. That week I spent time both with Phil and David Pawson (the other leader in the church), discussing what I had said and the way I had said it. We concentrated on content, approach, attitude, mannerisms, illustrations, phraseology and so on. I still have the two sides of foolscap paper crammed with closely-typed words and David's handwritten notes in the margins.

This sort of involvement in my apprenticing was to be the norm for the next two or three years. It confirmed to me how important it was that I should be willing to ac-

cept criticism, correction and help in every area of my
life. I didn't find it easy—in fact I began to dread it. I
could not seem to match up to what I thought was expected of me, and I wondered if my potential was ever
going to be realized.

The whole of the church's life at that time was mine to
learn from—worship, baptism, membership, finance,
decision-making, church government and structure,
youth work and relationships. I didn't have to agree
with everything; the important thing for me was to learn
from it all. Not only did this require my willingness to
get involved and to learn, but also the church's willingness to open up and let me in—which they did.
Throughout this period my loyalty both to the leadership and to the whole body of the church was integral to
my development as an individual.

Growing as an apprentice

When the church finally took me on a full-time basis in
1978, I had more time available to develop those areas
in which I was beginning to realize some potential. Although at that time I could not say definitely what my
ministry was, I was beginning to know what I liked
doing.

My involvement with young people developed and I
began to work in schools, taking lessons, assemblies and
Christian unions. They key to this work was the ability to
communicate and relate to the young people involved.

Schools work was very helpful to me and taught me
lessons that I feel are part of my life now. It took hours
of preparation which was a valuable discipline in itself. I
also had to battle through a personal difficulty I had in
approaching a school and asking the headmaster or
teachers whether they would be willing to have me involved in some way. When speaking to them I was conscious that my future in schools work depended on how

well I communicated with these people who had the authority to invite me in or turn me away. It was a pioneering situation, as was the sort of apprenticeship that I was going through in the church, and at times it didn't feel at all safe.

At church I began to lead services. At first this was under very watchful eyes and severe restraints. These restraints lessened slightly when I became a full-time worker in the church, but they were nevertheless very strong.

I was constantly aware that I was standing alongside men who were far more experienced than myself. Having been a member of the church for some time, I was also aware that we considered good organization and smooth running to be very important. Although I struggled personally to fit into this fairly rigid framework, I knew that if I could find my freedom under such constraints then I would begin to know freedom as it really is. Again, the way I conducted these services and what I said all formed part of the follow-up conversations that I would have with Phil and others in the leadership after the event.

With Phil's encouragement I began to get outreach going in the church. This continued and developed quite strongly when I became full time. Although the outreach was centred on the young people, as is often the way in churches, it provided extremely good training for me in how to organize outreach and communicate the gospel effectively.

This training climaxed for me when we had a major outreach, based at the church, into a number of schools in the area. There was a period of one week when, ably assisted by John Allan and the ubiquitous Ishmael, we saw some seventy young people come to the Lord Jesus. Consequently the number of young people in our church trebled.

One of the major difficulties I encountered during my

apprenticeship was working within restrictions and restraints. With each area of my involvement, Phil and I
would talk through how I had got on, what I should do
and what I should not do. There were things I needed
to hear and know—whether I liked it or not. I have now
come to appreciate the freedom I began to discover
from working within these restraints. It has given birth
to a very real creativity in a number of areas of my life.

Another major difficulty I encountered was how to
arrive at some sort of self-knowledge, and how to remain true to the person God had made me, while under
strong restrictions and constraints. Many times I felt as
if I was on the border of losing my own personality and
becoming a clone of someone else. I thought that if I
spoke and acted like those who seemed to be accepted in
the church, then I too would be accepted. I came to
realize that even though I differed in character and personality from many of them, God wanted to give me to
the life of the church and the life of the church to me.

It is important, then, that the one who is apprenticing
does not try to squeeze the apprentice into the same
mould as himself. I felt that Phil's desire was to see me
develop as a person. He himself learned the importance
of this while apprenticing me.

It was said to me on more than one occasion that my
opinions and strategies were inevitably going to be those
of Phil Vogel's. I could have taken this as a real compli-
ment, even though it was not meant to be, but for me it
only highlighted my personal struggle. I think it took
Phil some time to see the sort of person that I was and
the need increasingly to give more freedom to that person. Hopefully I was not what I always had been, but
was growing into all that I wanted to be. I had to learn to
stand on my own two feet and to be sure of who I was in
God, for there would come a time when the apprentice
would finish his apprenticeship.

We are all apprenticed to the Lord Jesus and so our

learning never stops, but the subject of this book is an apprenticeship which develops a calling towards a particular ministry, and it is to that apprenticeship I now refer.

Discovering the time when the apprentice has reached the end of his apprenticeship is not as straightforward as it may at first seem. When two people are so closely involved with each other it can be difficult to be objective about whether the apprenticeship should end or should continue.

Apprenticeship in industry is for a limited period of time, after which the apprentice is given a job related to the skills learned. In the church, however, we do not usually have jobs as such to do, or salaries to earn, but we are in the business of growing into maturity in Christ. The decision over whether we should be released from apprenticeship or not has to be made with reference to that maturity.

Phil knew that my apprenticeship was drawing to a close as I began to take on more responsibility in the life of our fellowship. Phil was our team leader and yet he began to ask me to lead our weekly team meetings. He also took a short sabbatical and left things mainly in my hands. In this way the scene was being set for me to move on from being an apprentice.

If I was asked to choose the most important lesson I learned from my apprenticeship, I would say it is this: importance of seeing apprentices develop fully as a person, not just in their gifts, aptitude or intelligence, but in their whole being. The value of the total person should be given absolute priority.

Hopefully I will be able to apprentice others as I have been apprenticed. Indeed I trust I am doing just that. I was given the freedom to make mistakes and learn from them. I was given the freedom to 'blow it' and to know that I was personally supported right the way through. That has meant a great deal to me, and I try to put it into practice daily in my relationships with others.

In allowing me to take responsibility for my life and work, Phil has encouraged me to take responsibility for others. And that, after all, is the work of one who is apprenticing—the desire to see every man and woman mature in Christ.